SANCTITY

MICHAEL BLUVAS

En Route Books and Media, LLC
Saint Louis, MO

En Route Books and Media, LLC
5705 Rhodes Avenue
St. Louis, MO 63109

Cover credit: Michael Bluvas

Copyright © 2025 Michael Bluvas

ISBN-13: 979-8-88870-428-8

Library of Congress Control Number: 2025946942

No part of this book may be reproduced, stored in a retrieval system, or transmitted in any form, or by any means, electronic, mechanical, photocopying, or otherwise, without the prior written permission of the author.

This book is dedicated to:

The Holy Family
Constance
Zachary and Bridget, Caitlyn, Michaela, Joseph, Will and Seth
Oliver Patrick
Mom and Dad
Patrick
Grandma and Grandpa Kerdikes
Grandma and Grandpa Bluvas
Mom and Dad Powers
Abbie Bluvas
Daniel Hadland
Christopher and Julie
Tiffany
Don and Cindy
Todd
All my Aunts and Uncles
All my Nieces and Nephews
All my Cousins
All of our Friends

And
Our Little Angel - Madeline

God Bless all of you!

Table of Contents

Prelude iii

Chapter 1: Setting a Fire 1

    Introduction 1

    Carryover 9

    Erasing The Truth 14

Chapter 2: Burning Me Down 27

    Scorched Earth 34

    Embers 39

Chapter 3: Our Lady 51

    My Holy Lady 51

    The Rosary 67

    The Fatima Prayer, Mother Mary to the 3 children at Fatima 76

    Devotion and Promises 85

Chapter 4: Rekindling the Fire 95

    Tables of Corruption 95

    Production 106

    Dangers of the World 114

    Mothers and Their Babies 118

    Creating Our Own gods 123

Face Value Idealism 127

Chapter 5: Fire Power 135

Reconciled 135

Come to Jesus Moments 141

White Dove... 150

PRELUDE

The Covid pandemic officially begins on March 11, 2020. Actually, I swear the virus hits me, and my son Joseph, in late November of 2019. Almost four months before it becomes a thing. One night, I remember feeling a "weird" headache coming on. I've experienced many headaches over the course of fifty years but never like this. My description, achy to ice picky at times, throughout my entire head. With my head feeling so heavy all I can do is rest it on a pillow to alleviate the nausea. Eventually, it moves through my entire body with a little bit of a fever and a little bit of a cough. I am down for about two days. By the third day, I feel better. Then back to normal by day four. No one else in the family suffers from any of these symptoms early on in the pandemic. And I forget this incident ever happens, until I begin writing this book. For truth, I have to be upfront about this.

My "fiery ordeal" begins with the Covid lockdowns. Late 2018 into 2019 presents me with some carryover. This time period has nothing to do with the illness. No. God, our Father, uses fire to burn me down. All of a sudden, the world "cancels" me completely. The world takes most of my savings as it scorches me. Then my ashes are sifted through and rekindled. My red embers are built back up to a fire burning in my heart for God. Under the love and mercy of Heaven, fire means judgment and justice. It can also mean the forever of hell, taking away everything that Heaven promises. Freedom of choice is the key. Say, "Yes!" Can I keep it? … My history proves otherwise.

This wrath brought upon us is more than an illness. We are not in control. Journaling begins in May 2020, proving we are dependent on our Father. My handwriting may look like gibberish to some, maybe at first, but it takes on a rhythm all its own. Going from one crazy event to another. Documenting all the crazy makes my head spin right along with our world. I have to keep it all in the moment, the right now; otherwise, it will be forgotten and lost. Because of this, I am writing this book in the present tense as much as I can. There will be some instances where the past or the future tenses better relate the subject matter. But the goal is to keep it in the reality of the present. This can't be forgotten; our souls are at risk.

The first three chapters take place from May of 2020 to June of 2021 with journal entries from this time period. My fire is described by Mother Mary taking over right away. The result of Her promise is quick in God-time, but not painless. My Holy Mother leads me back to Jesus. The last two chapters focus on what I still need to learn. This time period encompasses more recent journal entries and better captures the rekindling process and fire power.

Since Covid, I have become a sponge for knowledge about our Catholic Faith. I have always been an avid reader, increasing now ten-fold. Starting with the Bible, finding meaning based on questions I've had throughout my life. I take with me everything I've learned in Catholic school, and I listen attentively after prayer in the mornings. It's always good to read another person's perspective on a subject, then relate it back to your understanding within reason and fact.

I could tell this story with only Bible verses. It would still tell a story, but it wouldn't be completely mine. This would be taken as colder, asking where's the fire promised? And only relatable to a point. Being relatable is the power of understanding the Bible. The stories I write about filling the pages describe me now. Fully defining me along with the accompanying journal entries, producing where my mind is at the time noted. This allows for a pure definition that the reader can take in and digest. Read the book as a journal or a diary if you prefer. As harsh as it was at times for me to comprehend, it taught me grace and humility. A how-to-be-dependent-on-God-our-Father.

Many of the stories within are sprinkled with various accounting terms and definitions along with computer terminology. Be assured they are all simple concepts for accountants and non-accountants alike. These are what I've worked and taught for approximately thirty – plus years. Counting and explaining numbers can be fun, but I definitely prefer counting Rosary beads and praying for souls with reverence toward our Mother.

There are many themes flowing throughout this book. They all thread the stories of my life together woven into me. I didn't realize this until Covid and my journaling. Some are more evident, flowing like rivers, such as, … Fire, love and mercy, dependence, humility, the serpent, knots, goals, trust, and suffering. Then some are flowing like streams, including power, production, temples, a single dove, and surrender. All reach the ocean of Truth.

The themes present throughout can be broken down further, where volumes of books can be written about each one of them. The goal in this book is to show how God transforms me. Reinforced by the five chapters, outlining the steps He takes – Be aware I do relapse at times.

When I become aware these elements are available, I grab them up. Even the fire. I don't flinch but surrender to our Father. This truth is my faith. I use them to improve myself on my journey in finding Sanctity and ultimately Salvation.

The Bible verses used are taken from *The Ignatius Catholic Study Bible*, Second edition, Ignatius Press, 2010. Sometimes, I implement a small summary based on the explanation guide within this Bible as it relates to the subject I am presenting.

Catholic Online reinforces what I've learned about Catholicism through Catholic grade school and high school. A great reference to reinforce the Faith.

Chapter 1

SETTING A FIRE

Beloved, do not be surprised at the fiery ordeal which comes upon you to prove you, as though something strange were happening to you. But rejoice in so far as you share Christ's sufferings, that you may also rejoice and be glad when his glory is revealed.

1 Peter 4:12-13

Introduction

We are a month into this thing now. My job as a life insurance agent has been put on hold. My wife's job, well ... has been put on hold, too. Hers is officially a furlough. All I know, we aren't being paid. Locked down. One week ... two ... three ... then four. The question is, how long? Any longer, the bigger question becomes, why?

Journal Entry May 2020

God and Heaven are pure love and mercy ... Meanwhile, on the other side of Heaven, here on earth, He burns me down! Yes, the Father set a fire in me.

Setting me up for the "perfect" fire. My Father tells me, "I have too much invested in you!" Through my red, glowing embers, He sifts through my ashes, cleansing me, building me back up stronger, branding a scar onto my soul. I am His again.

His grace is there once more, providing me with another chance. It's not punishment for my sins, for Our Savior, Jesus Christ, already took care of that. It's the consequences of my poor choices I'm still making. Lessons must be learned this time.

St. Peter expresses the same thought above, sharing in Christ's sufferings, then rejoicing when His glory is revealed. A *"fiery ordeal"* reduces me to almost nothing in this world. It is not pleasant when this reality becomes the moment. But as a good father says to his child, "This hurts me more than it hurts you. Love and mercy insist on choice, judgment, then justice!" I understand this now.

My fire begins … late 2019 into 2020. We all hear rumblings of a new disease making its way from the Far East. All I know, it starts with the word Corona then trails off with the word virus. This isn't so disconcerting to me along with all the media hype because the carryover from the prior year presents more important issues needing my attention. My world is a knot, manageable but tight.

After the smoke clears, I can't believe how far I am pushing Him away. The right intentions are there, but I lose sight of what's really important. God entrusts me with some very special people, my wife, all my children, and eventually grandchildren in 2021. Instead, I spend most of my time working on earthly matters, saying, "I do it all for them!" Then more blasphemy, "Father, once I succeed, I will fully embrace You again!" Yes, I willingly give up my previously earned graces, all for this world.

Many times before, I act like a spoiled brat when punished. After my wounds heal, I follow the same easy path this world offers,

Chapter 1: Setting a Fire

further increasing my own stock price or learning how to do so more effectively. The space between me and my Father growing larger each time. I refuse to see what He has in store for me.

This isn't always the case in my life. Growing up in a Catholic family, I am drawn to Jesus and His Mother right away. In my grandparents' bedroom, I meet the large statue of Our Lady. I can only stare. She is overwhelming at first—so beautiful in pristine white garments underneath a light blue shawl and golden halo. She solemnly watches over me with a loving smile.

The serpent underneath Her terrifies me. It's what I see at the height of a three-year-old. Long and scaly. Its head, huge and ugly, with black eyes piercing through me. I swear it wants to pounce then devour me. The request goes out, "Please put the Holy Lady in the other room," whenever I spend the night. Interesting how this Holy Lady always returns the next morning.

With the help of mom and dad and Catholic school, I figure out the importance of these religious icons. Now I see our Blessed Mother keeping Her foot on the serpent's head for a reason. My enlightened view, telling me by Her assured face, She is in total control of the situation, protecting all Her children, protecting me, while the serpent looks very uncomfortable. My childhood at grandma's and grandpa's is like Heaven on earth for me. The statue of the Blessed Mother holding baby Jesus becomes my vision of peace and tranquility. I miss them!

Jesus of Nazareth premiers on television in the late 1970's. One of the best, most realistic TV series for its time. It presents a genuine picture of Jesus that so many of us have in our heads already after reading through the Bible. Perfect in both the portrayal and preaching. Each night of the series I get comfy, watching in my beanbag chair. It mesmerizes me, as if Jesus is personally asking me to follow Him, just like the apostles. His eyes focus on me when He asks the question, not blinking, patiently waiting for my answer.

Jesus becomes my friend, better yet part of my family. We forge a trust where I can talk to Him about anything on a personal basis, which will be necessary in the near future. He doesn't yell; He teaches me the right way. Tears well up in my eyes during the Crucifixion, hiding them from mom and dad. Then letting out a few at His Resurrection … professing my faith, saying, "Yes!"

Plump to big-boned is me as a pre-teen. It happens to a lot of kids growing up. This turns into my moment. Unfortunately, it is my world for about four years. Heaven turns into hell at school. Kids constantly laughing at me and ridiculing me. Many of my classmates, who were my friends just a few years ago, consider me a joke. All are making a name for themselves in the cool department. The worst is always the look of … "you're pathetic" … without even saying a word. Ok, I just agree and move on.

I am pretty easy going, but eventually the volcano erupts. Fat loser jokes have to go. These events turn into shoving matches. Fighting back for the first time lands me in detention. It starts with me pushing, him pushing back, me pushing harder, him pushing harder. We get tangled up. My right-hand slips and clocks him on the mouth. The kid can't believe he just took a shot from a loser. Once he sees blood on his hand, he takes off running toward the recess teacher.

Every year, the jokes go further. I find myself getting tag teamed by a couple, three, four, or even more guys. It's hard to defend myself when no one has my back. This leads me to covertly scanning the halls when stepping outside the safety of the classroom. Hiding in corners when necessary, speeding up when clear.

The endless threat is draining, nauseating when at school. My own little secret. Who do I tell that can really do something about it? Mentioning it once to grandma only put "worry" on her face. I don't like that look. Don't want to ever see it again. So, I always pretend everything is alright. It has to happen this way; I don't want to bother mom and dad either.

As embarrassing as this is, at least there is a bit of a reprieve at home, on weekends, and glorious summer vacations. Today, there would be a social media barrage – cannons firing twenty-four, seven. My burden gives me the grace to love reading, building plastic models, and playing sports by myself against the garage door, then eventually organized soccer and basketball.

"Canceled!" That's me 1970's style. I never can enjoy the fun stuff at school. Asking myself, "What about me? I believe I'm relevant and one of the class, too!" I grow up hiding in the corners and not liking most trends of the period. Fluffy hair, parting it in the middle, boys pulling out their pocket combs with handles, combing through their hair over and over and again. Entertaining all the girls!

I rebel against fluff. Parting my hair on the side, the left side. I become an old soul about twenty years before my time while being a teenager. Loving everything from prior generations before I was born. I see them as simpler, happier times. Probably not for some, but the fluff of this generation sucks for me. I have to go somewhere safe. Grandma and grandpa constantly bring up the old days. Staying up late with grandpa watching old movies leads me to older music, older movies, older stars ... Carol Burnett, Johnny Carson, and, of course, Elvis Presley, Dean Martin, and Dion. All members of my Heaven on earth.

I'm not totally innocent here. I admit, I do this sort of thing to other kids a time or two as well. Trying to earn my own street cred. Probably why I treat my younger brother the way I do. Like a mean bully at times. My point, it hurts when it happens to you. Hurting others, especially my own flesh and blood, hurts worse. Feeling the pain worse today than all I ever experienced while joked about and tag teamed. My brother suddenly passes away in 2010.

An event on the bus in junior high before drop off is big. It's customary for me to sit in the front of the bus where it's safe. Today, I have to sit toward the back, leery of a set of kids up front. I reluctantly get up for my stop, experiencing claustrophobia in the aisle. On a cold day, I am literally sweating, it's hard to breathe, with my mind going through all of the potential scenarios. None of them turns out too well for me.

Just as I thought, they all pounce on me right away. "Hey blueballs, get your fat ass outta here!" Quick swiping pangs to the back of my head sting when passing by them. Each take a couple more shots.

Walking stoically down the aisle, my eyes focus on reaching the open door to safety. I don't look at them or attempt to block their swipes. All I can think about is loving my neighbor in the midst of the storm. That *Jesus of Nazareth* thing. No matter what they say or do to me. Trudging ahead, trusting Jesus has my back this time!

This experience is the first taste of sanctity for me. Again, all in the moment. Our salvation lies in the sanctity we attain and keep. The sanctity we let ourselves gain by embracing His love and mercy

Chapter 1: Setting a Fire

then taking on our own cross. Our Father always gives us a choice. We need to take advantage of that added push He provides whenever it's there.

A couple of takeaways here: I wish bullying on no one. It's worse for kids today as mentioned before. This experience is the main reason I stay away from social gatherings with crowds I don't feel comfortable with, if it can be avoided. Always finding a seat with an exit strategy. Most wouldn't understand it all. Especially my continual dreams of searching for my classroom in the midst of a dark, dreary, rat-infested school basement … my classroom is up ahead with the light on, it's right there, close, but, I can't reach it. And I don't like calling attention to myself, whether good or bad.

On the positive side, this all teaches me confidence in who I am. Since "blueballs" is one of my nicknames, last time I checked they aren't blue, the joke is actually on them! That's my mentality … So what! And, I do like speaking in front of crowds as long as I have a message. Overcome by teaching accounting classes. I can do it, and the more I do it the more fun I have, but it takes a lot out of me. Afterwards, I'm totally drained. Family gatherings do this to me, too.

High school is me removing the term victim from my vocabulary. I am relevant. My wings grow, allowing me to mature and enjoy life. Sometimes a little too much. Gradually giving back to bullies when warranted or my mood demands it. Better yet, learning to just walk away … Who cares! Walking away with a smile, maybe a laugh … Have a nice day. There's power in kindness!

A little pamphlet explaining Fatima catches my eye one day in Religion class. I pick one up and leave it in my backpack. In study hall, I become bored after I complete all of my homework. No sleeping. On a boring day, I find the forgotten reading material. Mother Mary speaks to me while I read through the fifty or so pages.

In October of 1917, She appears to three little children, Lucia, Francisco, and Jacinta, in Portugal. Telling them they're saying the Rosary too fast. Our Lady says it fills Her heart with joy when the Rosary is said slowly, with meaning. She informs them all, "Warn the world of the terrible suffering My children will experience, consequences of their wicked ways, if they don't change. Follow My Son, Jesus. Tell them all to pray the Rosary!" World War I ends about a year later.

The little children follow Our Lady's request. My reading this pamphlet over one hundred years later is proof they did what they were told. When we continually say the Rosary and pray, our Mother promises us many graces. Believers will have peace and well-being. My take, just like at grandma's and grandpa's house.

My first complete Rosary is said after this. Getting through it is long and extremely difficult. I do it because of what was revealed to me through the pamphlet. Afterwards is the first time I push God away. The Rosary is too hard for me, staying focused and boring! Mother Mary would intercede for me in other ways over the next few years as I mature and become a man. I am Her child; She will never abandon or cancel Her children. I learn more over time as God's time is not ours.

St. Joseph guides me during this time. It's His turn, leading me to manhood and fatherhood. I fully realize this when my first child is born and while enduring my first marriage. As drama filled and chaotic as these two events are, it might have been so much worse with everything I was facing and the players involved. I make my choice.

Chapter 1: Setting a Fire

He guides me along, allowing me to pound nails into strong wood. Building my life from the ground floor up, the right way. My hard work has to support all my children and future choices. At times, I am permitted to yank out the loose nails, placing them in more prominent positions of strength. Other times, I have to move on after my screw ups, working around the originals.

I need help with a thought I have after praying the Rosary. My thoughts center on going to Mass on Sundays. A lot happens on Sunday, sports, meetings, some work, so I ask dad, "Why do we have to go to Church only on Sundays? Why not another day as long as we go?" We have family over for a family function. His message, "We'll discuss it soon!"

Carryover

When I was younger and needed money, I just got another job. Three or four jobs weren't uncommon for me. It was a badge of honor for me. In the hopes this wouldn't be forever. Now with no job, again, resting upon my other responsibilities, I say, "What did I do wrong here?! This was never part of my plan!"

Journal Entry June 2020

Remembering my question, dad takes me aside one day, explaining, "First of all, because that's what God requests. Sunday! Second, we can't just pick and choose what we want all the time. There's no order when everyone is allowed to do their own thing. We need to follow what God requests." I get it, doing it our way only leads to pushing Him away, more and more.

By the time I graduate with my MBA, find my dream wife, have all my big family, and get the ideal job, it is 2015. Able to take all of them on a cruise to the Bahamas. We are extremely happy being able to do this cruise about a year after we celebrated our ten-year anniversary with one. After a few days, I miss all of them, we both do. So, we pack them all up a year later and go to the same exotic beaches.

Approaching the towering ship from our van, we see it becomes larger and larger more majestic. I see the twinkle in all their eyes, the … "is this really happening" … on all their faces. They can't believe what they are seeing. Tears weld up in my eyes, reminding me of *Jesus of Nazareth*. Hiding them with sunglasses this time. No one sees me.

But the faucet of sanctity and virtue is at a trickle. It runs sporadically through the different stages of my life. I embrace God then push Him away. I push, then He pushes a bit harder as the faucet clogs up with worldly goals. I am working hard with my manager, making our company an even better high-performing company. Even promoted to a supervisor, manager after a year.

New CFO's can be tricky. Especially when their management team doesn't understand their hopes and wants for the future. Or better to say, when they don't have the ability to form a productive team. Instead, they throw out little snippets and catchy word phrases from the latest business book fad, expecting everyone to know them all. The CFO is placing their own rubber stamp on the process they're leading. Whether it's good or bad, necessary or not, that's just what happens. In many cases it's arrogance, even stubbornness. Trying to place a square-peg into a circle-hole stubborn.

Sooner or later, the management team under this person begins showing their worth, too. They have to. This means cost cutting and layoffs, even when a company is performing well. They have no choice; there's no time to bring up alternative options. Management is running scared at this point. When everyone hears constant whispering in the hallways with accompanying office doors shutting, beware of layoffs. It could be me! All I can do is stay positive, keeping my people busy. Not letting reason and logic become lost to the abyss.

With paranoia setting in, there are a couple of suggested projects I'm not going to waste my time on. And I don't, not happening. I'm paid to be upfront, relating my experience in a tactful, professional manner. Busy work and projects with no goal or end date in mind is a waste of time. Period!

Holding my people together, protecting them, becomes my primary job. I am lost in the transition. It is me slowly walking into meetings and executive offices with bad news, thinking about how to explain it. Either the numbers don't work, or the process is misaligned. A couple times a mighty roar kicks me out, suggesting I don't come back until it works! No reason why, no reasonable plan of action, "JUST GET IT DONE!"

Promoted in one year and fired the next. My boss gets it before me, along with a few of the management team. We are collateral damage, scapegoats of bad decisions from the top. All by a CFO, who lasts only about a year himself. Even though it's not fair, it's the life I choose in this world. The finger is given to the building many times when I drive past it.

During this time my daughter decides to live with me full time. I was divorced many years before. My wife and I are ecstatic as all of the unnecessary drama is always worrisome. Maybe this will stop now … nope!

One of the problems, the state is still socking me with child support. They always find me when I owe it, making it happen without a lawyer, but I definitely need one in this case to stop it. Or so they say? Even though my daughter is of an age where she has input on where she lives.

My thoughts immediately go to deadbeats, both fathers and mothers. Dads that can't be found and moms using their child support funds for their own satisfaction. My brain overheats turning into pure hate for these people! I carry this with me a long, long time. How can some dads not be found when the state always finds me? Why can't the state clamp down on these mothers' spending habits? Anyways … I have no say or control!

I'm thinking … I just got fired, a lawyer will cost money, this will conjure up drama from the past again, and my daughter could possibly "have to" do something against her will? She is at a good place mentally and doing great in school. This doesn't need to be messed with. So, the shakedown continues. More like legalized theft. All I know the state keeps taking our money. There should be some sort of savings account accumulating these funds for my daughter, right? Who knows, maybe she'll receive it one day?

There's my job, my daughter, and now my mom. Mom passes away in November 2018. It was kind of sudden, although officially

Chapter 1: Setting a Fire

diagnosed a few years prior. Liver disease cruelly sneaks up on you. No, she did not drink. Even though we joke about her vodka habits before this, it's definitely not funny now. By October, we are all called together by the doctor and the hospital staff, informing us she doesn't have much longer ... What!? Nah ... she's right here in front of us, laughing and enjoying her dinner.

It was terrible to lose mom. Preparing for interviews on the morning of her funeral was extremely exhausting on top of it all. I am drained. Late 2018 doesn't have too many companies hiring former financial managers for grunt accounting positions just to make ends meet. We get through it. Putting my arm around dad, hugging his head. My little brother was right there in the mix of sobs and tears. We say goodbye as the casket closes.

I lose another person dear to me that is in my corner, which is slowly depleting. Loving me, sacrificing for me, raising me to be a strong Catholic, through all of my selfish choices and angry meltdowns. My mom lived by example, giving me credibility to be me that I have taken for granted. There are times my gut tells me to call mom when an issue arises with the family. I dream she's still alive. She would say to me, "Love You!" ... more and more whenever we would end our conversations over the last few years of her life.

Lack of a paycheck is always a problem, bringing about many more issues. One on top of another. It's more than a knotted rope now, but that serpent I despised so many years before. It is encircling its prey, priming it for eventual consumption. Family expenses must be cut. How to make it fair when your children are caught in the middle? Not their fault.

Answer ... you become an insurance agent! They'll even hire me to fill their voids. An accountant by trade ready to serve customers with his salesmanship. The irony is too much. An assumed introvert, meeting with people, telling them all how he can help them financially.

It works! Early 2020, I recoup my lost salary and more with the payment schedule in place. Even declared, "Rookie of the Year" for 2019 in the Omaha office. Maybe this is my calling? Satisfying my wealth, prestige, and ego? I believe in what I'm promoting. LET'S GO ... 2020!

Erasing The Truth

"I will work harder!" Says *Jurgis Rudkus* to his new bride *Ona* in *Upton Sinclair's* book *The Jungle*. The new immigrants from Lithuania have it plenty tough in America during the early 1900's. Journaling events with accompanying thoughts open my eyes. Showing where I fit in, defining many things. Too much shut down, too much civil unrest, too much government, too much world, not enough God! Truth is becoming toxic in 2020. Me, too!

Journal Entry July 2020

Behind the scenes more and more people are infected with Corona Virus. The initial threat isn't totally understood. Then people start dying. Too many unknowns lead to treating the situation like a pandemic to be safe. All until the medical community can find some

Chapter 1: Setting a Fire

answers for us. This takes time, accumulating data, until "the science" can be explained. In March 2020, most states, businesses, and schools lock it down. We need answers!

The world is told that lockdowns, masking up, and eventual vaccines are all the prescribed methods mitigating unknown diseases. In this instance, working to some degree, now officially a pandemic named Covid-19, maybe not? Did it work for some people? Not for me to say. Everyone must follow what their own personal doctor says and then do it, not just watch what to do on TV!

But ... when mandated by local and federal government, and some nosy neighbors, to lockdown and mask up, combating cold and flu-like symptoms, where "the science" proves the vast majority of the public tolerates, along with all the other issues our country is facing, still facing, the situation becomes a powder keg.

A civil war, brother against brother, nosy neighbors against neighbors minding their own business, large cities against a host of smaller ones. The preventable powder keg just sitting there, waiting patiently for a match. Saying, "C'mon, light me, here's the wick, I dare ya!" The bluff is called, some unscrupulous politicians magically produce the match, some disingenuous media scooping it and taking the bait, lighting the fuse, and, during an election year ...

... KA-BABOOM!

The explosion shoots out numerous cultural issues affecting our country, still today. Maiming everyone, whether they officially contract Covid-19 or not. Blowing up what's left of the truth into a puff of black smoke … drifting away. We become shell-shocked, subject to surreal emotional overload. More political than ever.

The deaths as terrible as these are should never be diminished. But it's never good when emotion is taken advantage of, while not following through when "the science" has been fully proven. I am living proof, and my wife is, too; people suffer without contracting the virus.

Covid-19 gives this country a wake-up call. Reminding all of us, nothing in this world is ever guaranteed, no matter how hard anyone works or plans for the future. Hitting all of us differently. Some find much needed family-time, some find they never want to work or go to school again, some find their inner activist and are still rioting, some tear up the U.S. Constitution, some find time to finally read it, some lose their faith, pushing God further away, in essence "canceling" Him … But I like to think more give in to their faith, embracing our Father. Still not able to look Him straight in the eye when praying, but embracing Him all the same.

July finds many of us still locked down unable to work. Looks like this will be the playbook through the end of 2020. This stuff can't really be happening? But it is! Journal writing begins in May, and I keep it going. I'm not trying to find any answers at this point, only capturing what is happening. Proving the craziness. This confusing time has the earth encircling the sun in erratic fashion, causing my head to spin right along with it.

Thoughts fill the pages, emphasizing the three most important aspects of truth in my life. The first, my family. Second, our country with its exceptional aspects and its still to-do's. Third, and most important, the Church, Jesus gave us over 2,000 years ago. Truth lies in all three of these God-created gifts to us all.

Sadly, all three of these have a negative perception of some kind attached to it in our poisonous political environment. I am caught up in the monster people are manufacturing. We breath in the obnoxious, secular gas breaking down all three. Many of our victories in freedom and truth have been canceled. Placing us back in time before these were achieved. Like they never happened, erasing them. Only emphasizing where we still need to be. Allowing a new generation of activists and destructionists to make a name for themselves and riot in the streets.

My initial task is spotting conjured up outrage and emotion hiding the smudges left behind by erasers found all over the pages of history. Reason and logic tell us something was there because some of this has already been accomplished. This is the black smoke drifting away after the explosion.

Who gains from erasing known historical facts and a Church, God's Church, established over two-thousand years ago? Or, from keeping people at home longer than necessary, not allowing for school, work, commerce, etc.? Maybe the same type of political activists releasing a guilty "Barabbas" but crucifying an innocent Jesus in a different time. Allowing only the loudest and most obnoxious group to speak? As an accountant, I suggest we follow the money trail and the tyrants' corruption will become obvious. This appears to be the most reasonable way forward.

Upton Sinclair was a muckraker in the early 1900's. Different time, we, today can only read about. Living and working conditions were horrible, especially in the industrialized big cities. Even worse for immigrants finding their way and assimilating in America. His book *The Jungle* never mentions red carpet welcomes or comfortable dwellings in five-star hotels for these individuals just to keep up with a political agenda. But the writing does lead to an "awareness" of the terrible working conditions meatpackers and other workers had to deal with.

Sinclair makes a sound argument, writing a realistic story about the time period, finding a way to relate it to our country peacefully. He doesn't just accuse and apply derogatory terms to individuals or groups. Instead, he tells a realistic, heart-wrenching story. The truth and a solid argument will set everyone free … eventually! Read the last sentence again, I said, "The TRUTH!"

Immigrants flock to these type of jobs. *Sinclair's* writing exposes the harsh reality of the times. The point is we establish laws for better working conditions and better pay for all of these workers. People's lives change for the better, with this there is hope in our country. Still plenty to do, even now, but in America we need to celebrate this victory, and the baby steps involved. The U.S. is a work in progress, made up of many small blessings, such as this, over time.

Researching our history also leads me to *Alveda King, Martin Luther King Jr's* niece. She provides us some very profound wisdom – (1) *Listen to each other*, (2) *Empathize with each other*, and (3) *Celebrate our victories with each other*! Her exact words.

Ms. King's wisdom is heard on Fox News in the Summer of 2020. I listen to and read all media outlets, especially independent journalists. I have to; I want the truth or at least attempt to piece it together like a puzzle. Once complete, I glue the pieces together and frame them.

Chapter 1: Setting a Fire

Number (3) above hits home for me, bringing up the holiday, *Juneteenth*. I want more *Juneteenth*! It's a big deal for our entire country. It needs to be added to our list and celebrated by all Americans. One group doesn't own it, one country does. It's another turning point in our history, defining us more. Further strengthening our "amendable" Constitution and thus America's promise and hope. Celebrate, we as a country overcome this horrific evil, this victory!

More thoughts emphasize, ... this all comes down to politics. Both parties are searching for the "promised land" with their party leading the way. The parties are marketing emotional overload, tugging at everyone's heart strings. They place bets on never finding the "promised land" here on earth. They're right, and they want to remain relevant. Instead of embracing our Father in Heaven there's that grandiose golden calf. The shining gold puts the hope of riches in our minds.

With politics, everyone is playing with pure emotion. Leading us to the devil's playground. Where that snake and his friends live. I choose not to play in this arena. But yes I do vote. Politics stretches the truth further ... and further, hoping the rubber band doesn't snap. Kind of like what I am doing to our Father when it eventually snaps back on me. One group has a hard time telling the truth, and the other likes to make up the truth and of course vice versa. Then there are the weasels!

The political parties are too extreme. Right equals left, left equals right, which only equals *Crony-Capitalism*, or corruption (notice I said Crony)! A manipulation of writings and policies established that only excuse too much power for a chosen few – not part of our Father, our families, or our country.

Leading people has nothing to do with this stuff. Good leaders open up forums, gathering good ideas from everyone. Never shoving bad ideas or their face values down our throats, benefitting only a certain few. And great leaders make an effort to understand current events, not just sharing their face-value for a narrative only. We are thirsting for truth, but can't find it here on earth. It's always hijacked. We kneel down to the golden calf, refusing to bow down to our Father in Heaven. Unless a person thinks they're superior to a golden calf!

Jesus never does this. He never rams ideas down our throats or makes us follow strict, unreasonable laws. Religious or civic. Our Lord's intent is to simplify our Faith. Start with love and mercy then proceed forward. Law and order doesn't mean making new rules and regulations to attempt Utopia. This isn't Heaven.

Going further than politics. Journaling brings out the civil unrest, fake victims, and real victims. Example after example, proving politics is only masking a material danger we are facing currently. That is the fight between big cities and many smaller cities throughout our country. Two total opposites. Hedging the truth is done with something I refer to as Face Value Idealism and its narrative. The use of this technique affects our families, our country, our faith, and eventually our souls.

Face Value Idealism with a narrative is some of the truth of a subject, bubbling up to the surface. It's sort of making up the truth and sort of not telling the truth. Bottom line, it is an ignorance of history, emphasizing the right now in the moment. Or, intellectually dishonest. It's the new mantra used in modernism and politics today. My journal entries highlight this through many of my comments, finding this has "canceled" me, too. It turns proven facts into exploding emotions.

It's made up of what we see, what we hear, what we smell, what we feel, and maybe what we taste, again, right now in the moment. What's hidden under the surface is the important piece, telling the full story. Below the surface is where the entire truth, where the fireworks take place. We are taking the easy way out if only the surface is accepted as truth. There can be unintended dangers underneath if one's not careful.

Take a twenty-dollar bill. Its face value is twenty dollars, printed right on the bill. The holder can use it to buy twenty dollars' worth of a product or service. Easy enough. Here's the potential fireworks, what if inflation crops up and increases. If so, the twenty-dollar bill still has a face value of twenty dollars but won't buy as much of the product or service just purchased last month. Always a big deal for people living paycheck to paycheck.

The next month you see a commercial advertising what you just purchased a month ago. "Blowout deals for only twenty bucks!" If you are not aware you'll either need to go back to the ATM (I know a debit or credit card is the norm, but bear with me), obtaining more money to purchase the same amount of product or service, or purchase smaller amounts. Maybe obtaining more bills with the face value imprinted on them is not possible, creating a dilemma for a person when necessities are involved.

This is what many people don't get. They have a hard time understanding there is more than Face Value Idealism with its narrative in almost everything. Politics, money and investments, science, history, and of course our faith and religion. They can't get over themselves;

they only see the history attached to their own age in the right now. They refuse to see the history existing before they were born, or the technical aspects lying there dormant underneath the surface, the fireworks at play. Or it's quite possible they do understand this and are only playing suckers!

History is a story, whether good or bad, there's always more to it than how it ends up. Erasing inconvenient history to serve one's politics or to write books is more than corrupt; it's a sacrilege under Heaven. It's pouring a bucket of water on the fireworks below the surface that leads to the entire truth.

The Bible is full of stories and parables about how man can be prideful and corrupt at one moment in time then become humble and faithful the next, since the beginning of time. But God our Father is in control and evil is in the world. God's time is not our time. God's justice is not our justice. Throughout history, every segment of people has at one time, or another been subjected to some type of slavery or bondage. Or some -ism not allowing people to be their full individual self under God.

Highlighted by the story between Moses and Pharoah. Every Easter, Passover a network plays *The Ten Commandments* from 1956. Highlighting the Israelites were slaves for a period of time. They are shown working on Egypt's pyramids and infrastructure in the mud and the muck. Moses proclaims to Pharoah many times, "Let my people go!" Eventually, it happens. Then God's people screw up searching for the Promised Land, becoming slaves to their own golden calf and impatience. Such is evil and its minions!

Or my ancestors in Lithuania subject to Soviet rule (slaves to the state) and Czarist Russia before that. It's surprising my great grandfather was even allowed to come over to America in the early 1900s. The only thing we can do is trust our Father's Plan. All of us past and present have the weight of our crosses to bear with our Lord Jesus.

My point, there is not one Face Value Idealist individual or group of today that can go back to Soviet run Lithuania, Egypt during the captivity of the Israelites, or even the pre-1865 American South to convince the powers that be of the time to change their beliefs on how they rule, not a one. Proven by how difficult it is to stop people right now, today involved with slavery or sex-trafficking. Since we know it's wrong, why does it continue even today … Our Father will fix evil on His time with the truth. We can never fix a problem by using Face Value Idealism and its narrative. When using this narrative, we play God as a sucker, too.

Diving even further, think about this … there's nothing better than a dramatic "movie" pulling everyone into the story. The hero experiences dilemmas, nothing but bad news. How can the hero overcome all of this? Only the destruction of the entire world is at stake, that's all!

Full HD and cinematic surround sound put us right where the action is. In the comfort of our homes. Safe and snuggling up with our family in blankets, hugging our pillows tighter as the story unfolds. The hero's quest draws us in; we're even fighting right alongside them. Brace yourself; the end is near!

Of course, this is without any skin in the game. Except paying for it. A real-life entertainment extravaganza. In the end, after about two-hours, the world is saved from total destruction. Evil is obliterated. We can now let our breath out with one big … ahhh!

What if … evil isn't obliterated? The world isn't saved? Seems to me there will be a lot of disappointed movie watchers with upset stomachs from too much buttery popcorn wanting their money back!

This is the point when I realize I have pushed God aside. But His grace is always out there for everyone to take a hold of at any time. Even for those who had previously grasped it but lost their grip … God's lifeline is always within reach. Our Lady takes the lead as I simply start off by praying, one *Our Father*, three *Hail Mary's*, and one *Glory Be*. I begin embracing Her Son again.

This becomes a weekly, to every other day, then eventually a daily process beginning at 4:00 am. I say all of these prayers three times, putting meaning and heart into the words. Ending with *"Jesus, I Trust In You!"* Then I sit there in the dark praying for the *"fiery ordeal"* we are in to please come to an end. As the fire spreads, it becomes more than a process but a daily devotion.

My thoughts spill out all over my paper … a real-life war is going on with evil. We do have skin in the game. We've got to change our thinking here. Evil is in our neighborhoods, in our schools, yes, all over our world. We are all soldiers drafted by the Lord to embrace Him and push this stain out forever. That manipulative serpent is slithering around our families and our homes through the holes in our cracks of faith. Just like in the Garden of Eden. As relevant today as it was then, if not more. The evil one is desperate.

We are actually battling for our souls, unlike the entertainment we spend so much money on. Not just the earth is at stake; now it's "our" own Heaven and "our" own Eternity. A blip in time can make us or break us when it comes to Eternity. This is yelling, "BAYO-

NETS!" Better yet, saying our ROSARIES bead by bead, fighting evil in the cruelest hand to hand combat this world has ever scene. Just as we are fully behind our movie heroes, we have something better ... I think back to grandma's statute of Our Blessed Mother, placing Her foot on the serpent's ugly head, protecting all of us.

"I need to do more" is hanging all over me like a fog. Haunting me with the word "Sanctity." I've heard this word since Catholic school but I'm not sure what it really means. I keep telling myself, "I've got to find my Rosary and my Bible." It's just a thought always followed by the excuse, "It's been so long, I don't remember how?!" The fog is growing thicker.

Most people don't see this. Based on the words I write in my journal ... truth is being canceled. I am proving it! Whether that be by family and friends (they walk around whispering and shutting doors on me too), "the science", companies, our government, our history, or me just giving up. My sweaty, sleepless, rolling over and over nightmare becomes the words I'm writing. But more importantly, I ask, "What happens if God our Father cancels me?" This frightens me to no end.

When we push our Father away, we forfeit our virtue and buy into everything making up this world. Discipline and order deteriorate. We are adding to our clutter with unnecessary items. Unused stuff, boxes, and paper stacking up in our homes and our beings, our mind flutters constantly with worry. We end up surrendering our God given graces. All of us accept only the face value of a subject. The narrative becomes selfish, asking, "How does this affect me?!"

Why is all this happening? How can gifts from God our Father be bad? Please appreciate, these entities are never bad unto themselves. God didn't create them in that way. The caveat here, very important for everyone to understand … there is evil in the world. Read the prior sentence again and add to it … that serpent is real! Men and women surrender to this world and the evil one for whatever reason, pride, control, it's easier, it feels good, I want more, etc.

We are all human, following in Adam and Eve's footsteps under original sin. We get caught in our emotional overload, losing our reason and logic. He gives us all a choice. How's your eternity looking? Mine, not too good. But God's fire fixes everything. Just let it burn!

Chapter 2

BURNING ME DOWN

If the world hates you, know that it has hated me before it hated you. If you were of the world, the world would love its own; but because you are not of this world, but, I chose you out of the world, therefore the world hates you. Remember the world that I said to you, A servant is not greater than his master. If they persecuted me, they will persecute you; if they kept my word, they will keep yours also. But all this they will do to you on my account, because they do not know him who sent me.

Matthew 7:15-20

A Wonderful Life

Corona Virus and all the hype hits our home. It is a vicious illness no one saw creeping into our country and our world. How many infections, how many deaths, how many working families losing it all? Yes, the virus, but even more its surrounding paranoia has devastated us. The family is healthy, but the toxic environment totally wiped us out! Call the doctor …

Journal Entry October 2020

Most people should be familiar with the Christmas classic *It's A Wonderful Life* with Jimmy Stewart. If not, watch it! I was on the verge of a riveting "George Bailey" moment, ready to take me to some pretty dark places. Think of Jesus and *The Agony in the Garden*. For my situation, not even close. He had all the weight of the world on Him, and He is innocent. I only have my family, and I'm not innocent. This isn't the first of these for me.

But this episode throws a fast ball right at me even before entering the batter's box. I only have a second to react and dodge it. I had the belief these moments were well behind me with all my planning ahead. Nope! No official rules of etiquette here, telling me I will experience only one, maybe a couple of these hopeless moments during my life. If I remember correctly, "George" only experiences one. Then goes back to his wonderful life.

Instead, I hold my ground and wham, a thud to the chest. I'm not a baseball guy. Those are my wife and three boys. Baseball fanatics. So as telling as this scenario is, it's true. My breath is held up inside my lungs, with my frantically trying to pull it out and breathe in again. I can't catch my breath, the normal rhythm becomes erratic, falling to my knees, flopping around like a fish out of water. Whew, there it is. Breathe in, breathe out. And again. That's the way I feel, the world is knocking the wind right out of me!

We are anxious for my wife's furlough to end in late October. By all accounts, it is a go. Unfortunately, we are so far behind on bills and expenses, it becomes bittersweet. But it is necessary to begin the catchup process. Severance depleted long ago, 401k is bleeding red, while we pay only the essentials, like power and food. Tirelessly negotiating others, like cars and mortgage.

Chapter 2: Burning Me Down

My life insurance career, too good to be true at one point, is stagnant. Trying everything to meet with people over computer zoom meetings. Calling and calling and calling. This is where I have failed. It's working for others, but not for me. I ain't the super-powered salesman I thought I was, losing my "Rookie of the Year" status. The people I talk with are too leery about even meeting from a distance. The few potentials I scrounge up usually prefer to wait until our environment becomes more stable, back to normal. Not really remembering what normal is. A couple of them still wearing masks even when online. Putting an exclamation point on our current world!

Negotiations with our lenders are always ongoing. Now it includes our Catholic school payments, amounting to about $600 a month with discounts for three students. We reluctantly make the decision to pull them all out of Catholic school. There is no choice. They are enrolled in our neighborhood public schools.

One of the problems of the transfer is the fact that we know many of the parents at our Catholic school. Sports, coaching, parent nights, and fundraising. We know just about everyone, and the teachers know our boys. At least Connie does. We go from one school to two as the junior high is separate.

I have seven children. Raising six, you're never done. Over that time period, there is a big generation gap of changes in parent-to-parent, kids-to-parent, and the parent-to-school interaction. The respect aspect doesn't exist anymore. Today, it's more of an insulting diss. Everyone is about themselves trying to stay ahead and in control. Snobby more than anything. This rolls out into the neighborhood as well. Introducing myself to new neighbors whenever I can, going from hi, how you doing one day, to not even waving or acknowledging me the next.

Many of the parents don't take responsibility for their kids, believing their kid or even themselves are never the issue. All a kid has to say to their parents, "It wasn't me!" or "I didn't do it!" The gas lighter will go further and blame the innocent. The parent reaction, "See … my kid didn't do it, must've been your kid." No verification involved. Teachers remain hampered by rules and regulations in order to not get sued. My boys need to learn how to act by the example of their parents, teachers, other parents, and coaches, not contradictory mandates.

Kids today talk continuous smack, whether they're good at it or not. Look at all the sports figures and the movie stars, along with the YouTubers and TikTokkers. The special ones have gas lighting expertise, too, stepping away after they set the flame. Blaming innocents when found. My boys are no different in this arena. Great to excellent smack talkers, poor gas lighters though. It becomes very difficult when other parents don't live up to the accountability of our parent-pact.

The day Connie goes back to work again, we receive a visit from the sheriff. I see who it is through the front door and quickly collapse against the wall out of view. Feeling like a criminal, my heart pumping out of my chest, I expect a loud bang on the door with weapons drawn. "What the hell's wrong now? Just please be nice to my storm door!"

My mind immediately goes to paying child support for my kid living with me full time. She wants to; it's her choice. Too low on my list of essentials, so I take a couple months of a reprieve. With the bang on my front door, it is paid and up to date. There's always a time lag for payments to the state, though. It doesn't have to come to a deputy sheriff leading me away in handcuffs. With my daughter

Chapter 2: Burning Me Down

screaming, crying out, "That's my dad, I don't want to go back there … PLEASE!"

Child support is always a problem, more when showing delinquent for thirty days or more. Now this and other late payments are showing up on our credit bureaus. A big no-no in many employers' eyes, especially the state issuing insurance licenses. Explanations and excuses don't matter. A line is drawn, and it's extremely difficult to get back above that line again, proving you're not a deadbeat. Again, the face-value narrative is king.

Debtors and dead-beats were sent to debtors prisons in the past. Picturing myself in the stockade pillory. My head and arms locked. With any takers, throwing rotten vegetables at my face. Take that "blueballs" … see, we told you, you wouldn't amount to much! Splat … splat. Soft, rotting tomatoes dripping red down my face. Black, grimy lettuce sticking to my hair. And the taste of the concoction oozing into my mouth. Here you go, take a shot. Any takers? My mind is constantly right there in the moment.

As quickly as he appears, he leaves. I don't have to discuss anything with him, breathing again. An envelope is in the storm door from a credit company officially notifying us we are delinquent. Pay up or be prepared to be sued. "Good luck, join the club," I think to myself. All the necessary information to contact them is conveniently provided. Throwing the garbage at the dining room table with all of the other notices and mailings. This is my filing system.

I stop answering calls from our lenders, letting them all go to voicemail, which is loaded. But I still see the time stamp of who calls and when. And hear the beeps that never allow me to forget my predicament. Some call once a day, some two or three at various times.

Psychological warfare. I don't like cell phones to begin with, all solidifying my thinking.

I even stop calling essentials with a good faith check in. We are able to make vehicle payments each month, but not in full. Each payment taking us further into delinquency. It's all interest and the passage of time. Just like the Armageddon national debt spreadsheet. Second by second, million by million, it is a real-time update of how much our country owes in trillions. My moment gets to the point where it really doesn't matter anymore; it's hopeless! It might as well be trillions for me, too. Just put it all on my tab!

On a day I go into the office to scrounge up potential clients, I receive a call from Connie. She informs me, "Uh … there's a man here with a truck, uh … he won't leave … he's in the garage, not letting me close it!"

My mind is going a million miles a minute. It finally clicks, … "Oh no, they're repoing our vehicle!" My biggest concern is I'm not there to protect her because he was stalking her from the shadows of our neighborhood. The only thing I can do in the moment is ask her, "Let me talk to the guy!"

The repo guy is smooth. Telling me, low and monotone, he has no choice but to rack it up and tow it away. I fire back that our lender is aware of this delinquency and is working with us. I check in with them weekly, so I say. Calming voice contending right back at me; there's nothing he can do at this point. The account had gotten too far in arrears. I stay calm myself in the midst of my brain shifting red, overheating. All I want to do is punch this guy.

He gives me the number of who to call regarding this extreme delinquency. And a number and address of where the vehicle will reside. All I can do is say, "Go ahead and do what you need to do!"

Chapter 2: Burning Me Down

Like he needs my approval at this point. I hurry home to fix this unexpected but important issue.

Now we are without the use of a vehicle. The other one is leased by the same lender. As I pull into our driveway, my first thought is a question, asking myself, if the lender can repo Connie's vehicle, then what's stopping them from repoing this one, too? If that happens, we won't have a vehicle to get around. My brain tells me to mitigate the risk. Park this one two streets over then go into the house.

The next step is to call these vital numbers. After a fifteen-minute hold, the lender finally verifies the records. The lender informs me that the repoed vehicle is more than ninety days past due. So much for checking in and being proactive. They have been applying all payments to our vehicle now parked two streets over. My body begins quivering, and my teeth are gnashing.

I have to at least appear pleasant to the customer service rep. We need our vehicle back and our records updated. I am cordial but need a few seconds after each of my replies to gnash my teeth. Especially when I'm told we need a $2,500 wire sent before 2:00 pm today if there is any hope of us getting our vehicle back today. It's Thursday, if not today, next week and another $2,500 wire. Not a simple ACH as normally processed but a wire from a certain designated wiring service that only a local grocery store can accommodate.

Unfortunately, I have everything budgeted, keeping our mortgage current with a little bit of Christmas. Another $2,500 means no Christmas and potentially losing our home early next year. This I don't share with anyone, not Connie, and definitely not the kids. Not fair to any of them.

Dad helps us here. He gives me a check when I arrive at his house. I walk in, he sees my distress, he asks, "How is it all going?" I try to be stoic but just have to let it out, crying in front of him. Thanking him profusely, along with, "I've got two hours to cash the check at your bank and get the wire out for starters. Then, negotiate with the repo company!" It's 11:55am now.

"C'mon, just hit send. You've got my cash. You've taken my information. It's in the system!" My brain is storming purple, but I am pleasant and accommodating, not letting the clerk see one bit of my frustration. I've been here almost forty-five minutes now.

Finally … printing. It is official, the receipt is printing. The recipient has the wire, confirmed! It's 1:50pm. But I do see the clerk's eyes, saying, "You're pathetic!" My distant past haunts me again with his look. This time, he's not wrong.

We produce the papers documenting our vehicle is currently paid up to the repo company. It's Thursday afternoon, 4:45pm. We are nothing but grovelers in this environment. Right away we're hit with a sign in the lobby, … "See you next time!" Big and arrogant, saying the control lies with the repo company. Is this the kink in the chain telling us we can't get our vehicle back today? They're all moving pretty slow with those same … "you're pathetic" eyes. "Not sure if we have anyone to bring your vehicle up. I think they've all left for the day?!"

Scorched Earth

My strength and stamina are fading. It's like I keep getting punched … harder and harder. Each one knocks me off my feet. I need to be able to block them or duck once in a while. I'm too slow. These punches are coming way too fast for me. Each one lands a blow. I stagger and fall after each one. Today,

I just get hit and fall. I get up slowly. My worry is my lump don't get up no more.

Journal Entry November 2020

"Black" Friday is the day when most stores and shops finally report a profit for the year. People's Christmas shopping kicks in. All is good when "Black" ink is seen on a ten-key running tape; money is being made. Then there's the "Red" ink, meaning money is flowing out the door. People say in this instance, the budget is bleeding "Red" ink. The year 2020 is now referred to as "Red 2020" in our household! The ten-key tape is official, confirming to the world, we are healthy, but we are broke!

Going anywhere out of the house is a hassle. This time I take Connie's vehicle, proving it's ours again. We get it back just in the nick of time as the repo company locates someone to release it right before 5:00pm. Maybe I find a good spot in my heart for them, "Nah, that was terrible!"

On one of the rare occasions I step out, walking into the grocery store, I feel different than all of the other people walking in. Why are they staring? Oh, yeah! "Damn!" Reluctantly, I turn around, back to the car again. This is what they want. Out of the assortment, let's pick the blue one to keep everyone safe today. Now blending into the crowd isn't a problem.

Remember masks? Some will want to slap me, and others will praise me. I'm sure everyone remembers because it is our life for a while. Mandated to wear them. Everything focusing on 2020, even 2021 into 2022, occurs with masks involved. Kids at school, the teachers and administration, and the sheriff. The repo guy and his company are all in compliance. Then there's the tellers at dad's bank and the wire guy at the grocery store. All compliant, except for some rioters and sneaky politicians caught on video at times.

Every time I wear this thing, my glasses fog up. I still haven't figured out how to place the mask properly on my face, fully covering both my nose and mouth, without glasses fogging up. Not enough practice getting that perfect fit across my face. Usually, I fake a total cover up, letting my nostrils out just a tad in order to breath. Totally defeating the purpose of the irritating exercise.

I wholeheartedly agree, if … IF, "the science" says we are actually in a horrific pandemic, I will wear three or four of the darn things to at least help a little! At this point, I'm really not in a mood to discuss, since it hasn't gone down that way.

Inside the grocery store, I am picking and choosing "necessary" food items. My glasses still fogging up, but I'm able to manage the inconvenience. Wheeling and dealing, I'm in a rhythm walking down the aisles. I'll take one of those, not that, substituting this because it's cheaper.

Full bellies are made of pasta. Cheap, delicious pasta. Feeding everyone in our family for at least a couple days. I pick out spaghetti and bowtie. By my calculations this will give us four dinners. Maybe, ham sandwiches in between. There you go, ingredients for a week's worth of dinners just like that.

Moving on from the pasta aisle there is a lady peering at me through her double mask and glasses. They aren't fogging up. She's got to be a pro. The woman is in the middle of the aisle and taking mental notes. I intend moving right on by her.

Chapter 2: Burning Me Down

"Excuse me, uh, sir ... ya know, you're mask isn't on properly!" I hear the woman, thinking she's speaking to another behind me. "SIR!?" There's the fire in her belly, her passion now on display.

"Oh, you're talking to me, I'm sorry." My eyes telling her, please repeat.

"I see your NOSE! I'm not supposed to see your nose!" Her eyes telling me, comply or else. Her mask gives this little old lady added credibility, projecting fear and apprehension to all non-compliants. More zombie-like if nothing else. No fear here, since I'm already another case of collateral damage from our meddlesome, power-hungry environment.

Oh, I got it now! You're one of those. She can't see my mouth and jawbones clenching. As she says nose the way she does, my response loads into the chamber. My eyes are looking at her as merciful as they can with what's about to hit her.

I explain, "I wear shorts, gym pants, or khakis along with my briefs of choice every day. Ya know what?" Not actually waiting for a reply, pointing my head toward her, eyes not blinking. "My family complains—they can still smell me!" Not the right way to handle the situation but my anxiousness or whatever has been nudged.

Out of respect, I pull my mask over my nose fully in compliance and say, "Make sure to stay six-feet away from me, please!" Making hand motions, identifying about six-feet.

The cashier quickly scans my grocery items, finishing up with the milk and a couple bags of price shattering cereal. The register doesn't print this time; it's thinking. I know there's plenty of money in the account for this. "Or, do I? Ahh ... C'MON!" The cashier, waiting customers, and even "mask" woman off to the side with all their proper masks give me their ... "you're pathetic" eyes.

I definitely can't argue with them at this point. Breathing more heavily my glasses fog up even more. The store keeps the cheap cereal. There it is, finally, the sound of printers completing my transaction. I yank my card out, shaking my head. I can only leave the store with what I can afford, going home to make dinner and figure out how much money is left.

Ripping through the pile of mail on the dining room table, envelopes, statements, notes, you name it, takes about two hours. I find the receipt plain as day on the table next to my chair. "Oh yeah …!" It's that check I wrote just a few days ago. Depositing it at our other bank. We need that $100 bucks so our utility payment will go through.

Looks like we use only one bank now; keeping two is impossible. No more screw ups; we need at least one bank with no issues to draw upon. My mind is overloaded with issues. Now I have forgotten something that happened just a few days ago. My account was off by only $5.50 … might as well be $1,000 at this point.

The crafty serpent is fully wrapped around me. I keep thinking I can stay one step ahead of it. Instead, it gets into my inner circle. My life and family. It's taking my time, my mind, and my body. I can't breathe anymore; it's pulling me away from … me. I understand this thing has always been around, from my early days at grandma's house to becoming a man.

I sure got ahead by pushing God away, but at what cost?! That serpent is uglier than I remember. "Grandma, please put the Holy Lady in the other room," I remember saying. Can't happen now. I'm the one that let the serpent in. Now, I have to kick it out before it consumes me. It's bankruptcy time.

We need the zoom call with our lawyer and the bankruptcy trustee to go well. "It's a go" is the best news we can hope for based on the current financial state we are in, with the ability to pay it all back. No reason to be nervous, right? Creditors will have to cease and desist any contact with us. They'll all get their money back, which is the way I want it, too. Hopefully, we won't be living in a cardboard box on the side of the street ... at least for now. Bless those that have no other choice.

Embers

I don't expect much from this world anymore! I am bleeding out, "the science" is prickly, continually severing me. Each cut forcing out a painful groan. Don't expect or plan on the secular, it will only disappoint. This world and I have never really gotten along. It is official, I have nothing left to offer this world. The world has taken it, I am not me no more ...

Journal Entry December 2020

After a fire scorches a forest, embers are always shining bright red hidden within the ashes. That's why fire fighters are on call to monitor the situation. There is still so much green life and seedlings hiding beneath the ashes and the embers, so the hope is within a year or two the forest will be green and vibrant again. In this case, Jesus is my fireman going through the ashes, seeking out embers that can be refurbished.

There is a stark difference between a destructive fire, scorching the earth, and a peaceful white dove, replanting the seeds of hope.

Nothing new here; this is Jesus working His Spirit through His Mother. All part of the "greatest story ever told." I am part of that story.

Jesus tells me as I listen in the dark, "Find My Mother and you will find Me. She will lead the way for you." Truer words have never been spoken because He actually saves the world, delivering us all from darkness. Saints and popes agree. We need to embrace Our Lady, picking up our own crosses. Now we have skin in the game!

The zoom call is successful, alleviating some of our mental anxiety. The dilemma becomes manageable going forward. There's some hope for the future. In return, the powers that be complete the "cancelation" process and designate us officially bankrupt. But then, we aren't hit with two or three or ten weekly, or even daily, emergencies anymore. The transfer of wealth from us to this world has occurred, pending a five-year payback period.

Late 2020, I am officially broken, my mind, my body, … my soul. Almost nonexistent. The draining year has me now searching for answers as to why all of this happened? How to accept it and then cope. Haunting me is that pesky word "Sanctity," once more.

December 20, 2020

Haunting isn't the right word. Maybe I should say, lingering, yeah a little bit … or irking, yes at times. What I can say is that it is persistent, and it is inhabiting me. What does this word actually mean? I ask this even though I've heard it since Catholic school.

Pillaging through a couple bookcases, I find my dictionary. How does this world define it? I need to know, now!

Saintliness or holiness, the fact of being sacred or inviolable, or anything held sacred. Synonyms include: holiness, godliness, blessedness, saintliness, goodness.

Webster's New World College Dictionary

Sounds like a good thing, right? ... Always depending on who is asked. The only problem is, this ain't me. Reminding myself, I'm a sinner, I don't follow the Father all the time. I don't think I can?! "Please Father don't 'cancel' me. I have nothing left to offer my family or You. I am sorry, so very, very sorry. PLEASE help me?!" Tears running down my face, I feel empty.

"Wow ... there's my Bible!" Looking at it for a second or two, realizing it won't shock me. I grab it. Sneezing after shaking the dust from the pages, the seismic interruption blowing up the tears. I see mom had signed it in red on the first page. "To Michael Gerard Bluvas, Love Mom and Dad, 1981." "Oh yeah!" ... Remembering the happy thoughts with all of us together at Christmas that year. Leading me further to, "What does the Bible say about sanctity?"

Before answering, my eyes automatically find my rosaries on the shelf above. The black beads appear gray, but I don't sneeze this time. This one is a gift from mom and dad, too. From the Vatican store. The Our Father beads state the specific mystery in words, all fifteen.

"And such were some of you. But you were washed, you were sanctified, you were justified, in the name of the Lord Jesus Christ and in the Spirit of our God." The point is that God's grace and forgiveness can rescue even the worst sinners from their deadly habits. The effects of Baptism: washed … justified … sanctified.

1 Corinthians 6:11

I don't stare this time, grabbing it immediately. After cleaning the dust off, I place it on the table on top of my Bible and journal notebook by my chair in the family room, along with my "How to pray the Rosary" prayer card used over twenty years ago during my "Holy Hour of Adoration." The table is cleared of all clutter, trash, cups, and bowls. I want easy access to answer my questions. Everything I need is right there now, as it had been throughout my life. This is the persistence, or driving force, only a mother can answer for me!

December 21, 2020

My eyes abruptly open as I immediately grab for my cell phone, 3:58 am. The 4:00 am alarm is turned off. I'm not tired but excited. Rolling out of bed produces a clean face and clean teeth. Then coffee and my chair. I pick up my Rosary with prayer card, turn on a small light and the TV. Turning on the TV is my go to, always, and it takes over my attention. After a few minutes, I turn down the volume. Then, I feel the need to turn it completely off. I oblige.

Saying a full Rosary this morning is the goal. Monday's emphasize the five *Joyous Mysteries*. I start off slowly, reading along with my handy prayer card. I'm feeling a little awkward, more like clunky. Eventually, I keep a rhythm between reading my prayer card with my left hand and moving my fingers along the beads with my right.

Chapter 2: Burning Me Down

The first two Mysteries, *the Annunciation* and *the Visitation to See Elizabeth*, find me increasing the speed with which I say *the Hail Marys*. I don't have to read this prayer because I've said it so many times throughout my life, realizing now, still not enough. Touching the beads faster and faster with my built-up energy like a machine gun aiming at the devil but missing it without a scratch.

I catch myself with *the Birth of Jesus*, the third Mystery. Saying this Mystery and the fourth, *the Presentation in the Temple*, slowly with meaning from my heart, like Our Lady requests the three little children of Fatima to do. The right way allows for larger shells to target evil, disrupting its legions all around me, making Her smile with Motherly affection as I honor Her!

Saying the fifth Mystery, *Finding the Child Jesus in the Temple*, is game changing for me in terms of my faith. Beginning with the first of ten *Hail Marys*, I sense an inner ecstasy, a state of pure joy far greater than I've ever felt before, even when drunk. Greater than being married (the second time). Greater than being there for the births of my children. I feel my heart and mind in union with my soul, each balancing the other. I am smiling with so much love for my Blessed Mother. In the dark with eyes closed, I see Her outline sketched out in blue.

After the tenth *Hail Mary*, my state of joy winds down slowly to almost normal. My shirt is soaked. After saying the *Hail Holy Queen* prayer, a headache develops from the stark contrast in what must be a piece of Heaven and then back to this world again. Maybe a hangover? But I don't mind. Everything appears right with the world now. I remain in my chair in the dark listening.

My mom pops into my head, then my brother, then my grandparents. I hear each of them just as if they are all mixing it up at a family gathering. There's some laughing mixed in, my heart melts with nostalgia. But I have a hard time seeing them. I know they are all good people and follow the Lord. I remember their goodness, as each voice reaches me in its own unique way. This time no worry in grandma's voice.

"Where are they? … Blessed Mother, where are these important people in my life? I have to know they're all ok and under Your Son's Divine protection? Please enlighten me!" Listening more intently, waiting, I don't hear an answer to my question.

Darkness can actually be scary, too. Without full faith and belief in Jesus, it can be downright frightening. For no reason, I feel my throat drying up and closing shut. The path to my lungs is shutting down. I can't swallow, and I can't breathe in or out. Without this world's oxygen, it only takes a few seconds for panic to set in. It's getting tighter and tighter.

I can't scream or make any type of noise out of my mouth. No one is up yet; they're all upstairs sleeping. The only thing I can do is knock over some of the clutter that has built up since the time Covid started. I kick some boxes over behind my chair. This makes some ruckus, but not enough to awaken anyone upstairs.

Don't know how, just did it, I grab my rosary and run to the bathroom. Turning the faucet on. Frantically, attempting a breath. Even moving my head and neck around. Maybe these antics will loosen up my throat for a little bit of air. In the mirror, I can see my red face turning more blue … I'm going to pass out!

I hold up my beads, but my strength is fading. Part of the Rosary falls into the sink, but I'm keeping a tight grip on the crucifix. My last thought, throwing myself against the bathroom wall. Back first. In my head, I say, "Please, Jesus, help me!" Once, nothing. The second

Chapter 2: Burning Me Down

time, even harder, "Poooph," breath comes out. Immediately, I breathe in a huge gulp of air. And again, more. And again, even more. Finally, almost coughing up a lung.

> Submit yourselves therefore to God. Resist the devil and he will flee from you.
>
> **James 4:7**

The mirror documents my blue face dripping with sweat and angst. I sit down, telling no one. I don't have asthma; I've never experienced this before. I let it slide. Thank God I beaded up, taking my Rosary with me. Whatever happened did not like my Rosary or me saying the prayers! "I think something just tried to choke me?!"

Going forward, every time I choke or have a coughing fit, I panic in the back of my mind, thinking, "This is it!" I also condemn others, which I shouldn't, asking, "Are you ok?" I know they're only trying to help and console me. But, because of my experience here, I don't want the attention drawn to me. I hurriedly pick it up and move to a quiet corner to handle my business. This is one of the reasons I carry my blessed pocket rosary with the "miraculous medal" always attached to it.

I wonder, "What if this event had killed me?" No one would be any the wiser because evil would have succeeded in taking away a husband, a father, a grandfather, a son, a brother, a friend. All because this guy is trying to get back to Jesus after leaving Him. It would also leave me wondering, "What's Jesus going to do with me? How much purgatory? ... How much hell? That's eternity, too, right!"

December 22, 2020

Tuesdays tell the story of the *Sorrowful Mysteries* when saying the Rosary. My eyes sharply open, and I see 3:57 am on my cell phone. This morning I'm a little timid with what happened yesterday, but I do get down to business. The TV isn't turned on or even acknowledged; instead, my family is still taking up my thoughts. This replaces the haunting of the word "sanctity" as solved previously.

The Rosary is said with meaning from my heart, keeping the rhythm, bead by bead. Each *Hail Mary* projecting love and devotion to Our Lady. Beginning with the *Agony in the Garden*, the *Scourging at the Pillar*, then the *Crowning with Thorns*, through to the fourth Mystery, *Jesus Carries His Cross to Calvary*.

From the outset, I feel the ecstasy of Heaven building up again to the fifth Mystery, the *Crucifixion and Death of Our Lord Jesus*. It consumes me again with my first *Hail Mary*. Eyes closed, I see Our Lady, outlined in blue again. This time, I feel the hand of Her Son on my shoulder, too. A little piece of paradise here on earth. I'm smiling, not wanting it to end … as it eventually does after I honor Her.

Sitting in the dark listening, the joy I felt just a moment ago muffles into a dull disturbance throughout my entire body. Going from a piece of Heaven back to the reality of this world, I tell myself, "I don't think I can handle Heaven on a permanent basis!" But I savor this gift. My eyes close. I fall asleep.

After a period of peace and tranquility, my eyes pop open. I hear, "Daddy … Daddy!" from a soft, angelic voice I'm not familiar with. I sit up, staring into the dark, dazed. Then looking on both sides of my chair, panicking, rummaging around for a little one that's lost.

Chapter 2: Burning Me Down

There she is, she's right there, I just heard her, right there! I'm gnashing my teeth.

My eyes close again. I see all of the people I have been concerned about. Bright, clear, colors like technicolor in the 1956 movie *The Ten Commandments* appearing in a picture perfectly hung in my head. Better than a Michelangelo. Forming a current portrait of a piece of Heaven with my Mom, Patrick, Grandma, Grandpa, and … Madeline? My mom is holding her grandchild with Grandma looking over.

Madeline, our little one, passes after twenty weeks. I remember telling my brother Pat at the time we were pregnant, which is our last conversation between him and me. A couple months after Pat passes, she is born, early, too soon to survive. Our twin boys are born a year to the day the following year. That's the soft voice I hear. I've found her.

All smiling as if all their worries are gone. They look their best, young and vibrant as I remember, dressed in nice Sunday clothes. Mom in a blue dress and veil with pearls, and Madeline in her white Baptismal gown. Grandma next to her, same dress but a lighter blue with matching veil and pearls. Her added eye squint isn't worry; she just can't get enough of her new little great grandbaby. Patrick in a dark blue suit just like high school graduation. He now has eternity in paradise in front of him, not the disappointment of this world. Grandpa has a black tie with clip on top of a white sleeveless button down; yes, his mischievous grin is showing. And my dad's parents, Grandma and Grandpa Bluvas, directly behind them. They all have what looks like the Celestial Court of Heaven as a backdrop.

After the picture they're all invited to an outside picnic. A beautiful Spring day, sunshine, no clouds, no bugs, and not too hot. Otherwise, my mom and grandma wouldn't be outside. The colors of

God's creation are spectacular. Looking out at the hills of grass and trees, so many greens, yellows, and browns our world of crayons can't define. Contrasted by the brilliant blues of the sky. No clouds. Our Father, the Creator is the full power of the sun, reflecting His glory. All of the white, yellow, golden rays shining brightly from Him. No shadows. His light touches everything, like a colorful stained glass window telling the story. Jesus and Mother Mary coming forward to greet us all with smiling faces.

Our Lady answers me! … I can't stop crying. My nose is stuffed. No sniffling or blowing. Again, I run into the bathroom, trying to be quiet. I close the door, turning on the sink faucet full blast. Sweet water running. Buckets of cleansing tears flow into the sink and onto the towel, dousing out any of the remaining used embers. The towel muffling my sobs. After I gain composure, it is soaked. Looks like Sanctity is beginning to flow freely?

Looking in the mirror again this morning reminds me of yesterday. I look a mess. But at least I'm breathing and not turning blue. I guess this is what a miracle from Heaven looks like and feels like when it wins a hand-to-hand battle with evil. There's so much well-being, happiness, and love flowing into my soul. Burning fire is taking over my heart.

Why do I cry? Is it for me? For them? Am I scared? Probably a little of all three. These people are my family, part of me, still building me. Not the canceled me before the fire being burned away along with the excess of pride, arrogance, and blasphemy. Our Mother, now allowing me to see all of them clearly, hearing them, appreciating them more. Her Son placing them in my life, moving me toward something I didn't think I could muster … Sanctity.

I learn that sanctity is trusting and embracing the Father on earth. Hope out of darkness and despair. Heaven and Eternity on God's terms. A holiness developing after He breaks down the arrogant self for its own good, after making some bad choices. Then realizing what Heaven and Eternity mean, squeezing our Father tightly, taking advantage of His graces, not letting go, forever. Picking up our own cross through all the good times and bad. Finding its building blocks again, consisting of virtue, discipline, order, and accepting God's grace.

The evil one doesn't like God's children on earth obtaining or keeping Sanctity. Desperation leads it to doing more advanced diabolical things to people. Unfortunately, people let it in. It's not just going to slither away without a fight.

How do we keep Sanctity? How do we get it back when it's lost? How do we save souls? Let's go on a little ride, my ride taking me there fast. Let's start our own fire in this world like Peter and Paul. Allowing the Holy Spirit to fill our voids and dwell within all of us!

Chapter 3

OUR LADY

When Jesus saw his mother, and the disciple whom he loved, standing near, he said to his mother, "Woman, behold, your son!" Then he said to the disciple, "Behold, your mother!" And from that hour the disciple took her to his own home.

John 19:26-27

My Holy Lady

Prayer (Saying the Rosary) is the only real thing that doesn't knock me down. I cling to it because it helps, it deadens the pain, giving me a boost, helping me pick up my own cross. Sharing in the suffering of Jesus. Why can't people see this? Why did it take me so long? Our Blessed Mother will always lead us to Her Son. Embrace Her!

Journal Entry January 2021

Sharp discomfort shooting down my right knee is telling me I'm getting older. Time is running out, only adding to my anxiety and hopelessness. The crooked knee is bone on bone. No supporting cartilage, only agonizing pains. Spreading down into my calf muscle, extending further to the ankle. Making my entire body achy and sore at times. I walk on my toes with a limp, not able to place my right foot firmly on the ground. Interesting how one area of pain reaches my entire body.

The uneasiness becomes my normal. I'm used to it, taking into account whenever I go somewhere or play with the boys outside. Using my mom's old neck massager on my calf, pillows, knee sleeves, and tablets of Tylenol all appear to mitigate some of the discomfort. I get through it. Why not have a doctor look at it to properly diagnose the problem? Don't know, I'm a man with other more important issues. The pain is draining, and it's extremely hard to muster up energy to get up at times. I can't get back up from a sitting position without using my arms against, hopefully, something solid, hoisting myself up into walking position.

Since the time of my journal entry of note, I have had my knee replaced. After eighteen months, it feels so much better than the painful description provided above during Covid. See how Our Lady works. My job is to make the decision to get it fixed. It is a miracle, not directly but indirectly. I still rely on Her, "something solid to hoist me up." It's simple, Our Mother leads us to Her Son. Say "Yes," then pick up your own cross and follow Him. A lot of us aren't there or even close. What does it even mean?

After my knee surgery when I am lying on the bed in recovery, I remember coming out of the anesthesia with the *Hail Mary* on my lips. I keep saying it over and over again, just as I do every morning. It is definitely a habit now.

Remembering *Jesus of Nazareth*, the time I say, "Yes," to Jesus when He asks me to follow Him like His apostles. We become friends. I can talk to Him about anything, good or bad, without yelling. At least on His part. He understands and wants to help, but I need to pick up my cross, too. Unfortunately, this world has gotten in the way of that relationship. How busy I am at various times in my life is what decides whether I fully embrace Him or not. I am lost! To keep God's graces you have to say, "Yes" every day.

The relationship I have with My Holy Lady begins with the statue in my grandparents' house as mentioned in Chapter 1. In the moment of being three, I remember being introduced. And, right away, my first thought is to ask grandma to place the Holy Lady in the other room when I spend the night. The serpent underneath Her foot is directly looking at me level with my three-year-old eyes. That's what frightens me. Even as a youngster, I see evil locking in on me.

She reappears the next morning. Always! The consistent event I grow to depend upon. I can only see Her solemnly smiling in full glory during the day. Darkness still puts me in the mindset of the serpent. I can't see beyond this; the moment is there, but the truth and true faith are going to take a while.

Hail, Holy Queen, Mother of Mercy! Hail, our life, our sweetness, and hope! To you we do cry, poor banished children of Eve; to you we do send up our sighs, mourning and weeping in this valley, of tears. Turn, then, most gracious Advocate, your eyes of mercy toward us; and after our exile show unto us the blessed fruit of your womb, Jesus; O clement, O loving, O sweet Virgin Mary. Amen.

Hail Holy Queen

After a year of fire, burning me down to scorched earth, my red remaining embers need this prayer. Yes, it's part of the Rosary, towards the end, but for me it's a beginning. This is the perfect definition of a new beginning with the help of My Blessed Mother. She is hoisting me up, with something solid, leading me to Her Son, Jesus, again.

Behind the scenes, both my mom and grandma provide firsthand examples of being a mother throughout their lifetimes. What mom provides to me, grandma doesn't. And vice versa. Grandma, grandpa too, spoils her only child. Most parents do. Nothing negative here. Her daughter is a princess, but her grandsons are kings.

Grandma is the doting mom, kissing boo boos, saying everything will be ok by hugging the bad away, going overboard on gifts, especially birthdays and Christmas. Worried about anything and everything affecting her baby. Noted by the famous "worry" look that she expresses through her eyes at times. Pulling her entire face downward. This is the look I never, ever want to see. Driving me to make her happy with a smile. I love when the smile takes over that look.

She is over every day when I am a youngster. She drops grandpa at work about four in the morning, then comes over for the day. She is always there when we go out for the day. This includes mom, grandma, me, and, eventually, Pat. On grandpa's days off, it is both of them as we all play around.

My brother Pat joins the Marines right after high school. He leaves for basic training before Christmas in 1987. We all gather and open early presents for him. After the presents, the rest of the family gathers in the kitchen and dining room to eat. Grandma goes down the steps into the family room to be alone. She doesn't notice I am still in the family room cleaning up some of the discarded wrapping paper. Once she sees me, she bursts out crying, uncontrollably. All I can do is give her a great big hug and try to calm her down. The "worry" look is covered up by her tears. Her heart is almost broken in two.

What Grandma doesn't know is that I am thinking about joining the Army. Entry for me wouldn't be until April 1st, basically April Fool's Day with all of the grown-up drama I am facing at the time. She would have passed right on the spot if I mentioned this in any form to her. Somehow, I think she knows this secret already.

A couple months later, grandma is in the hospital. Her heart and blood pressure remain out of whack. Her having been there a few days already for observation, mom and I go up late one night, the second time that day. Grandma actually looks relaxed, laughing with us and freely talking about good times. No "worry" look evidence present. This puts us both at ease after we leave for the evening. Mom calls early the next morning a little after four, "Michael, grandma's gone!" She says between sobs. Grandma has a stroke. She will never experience her "worry" look again.

My mom loves me just as much, but is not as emotional, except when she gets mad. Not mad but … MAD! Always a good trait to have when in my corner. Not so much when on the other end, facing it. After her explosion, she becomes quiet for a bit then she quickly returns to normal. This persona is me to a tee. More practical than grandma, always sticking to Catholic values. Leading me through Catholic School, the sacraments, and Catholic high school. I think of the fourth Joyous Mystery, the Presentation in the Temple, and leading me in the duties of our faith that Our Lady shows us.

I am two-years older than Patrick. After my high school, I go on to college the next semester and work as a runner for my uncle's law firm, covering some of my expenses. Saving money is also a goal of mine, so I take on a second job, night stocking at a grocery store. Doing this allows me to save money and build up some cash for a new stereo catching my eye. I figure maybe a little over six months, and it's mine.

Working and school, plus a little bit of going out with friends. All ok because you don't save much by partying it all away. Partying is still in the budget though, only sometimes. After about three months, mom notices my schedule and asks me about it. I tell her my plans. About a month later, out of the blue she tells me, "Go ahead and get your stereo … your dad will pick up the rest of the cost for you!"

Wow, "That's what intercession means!" Yes, that's what happens with "Intercession." Mom sticks up for me. Not that dad doesn't, but mom just knows and brings the subject up to him. After this experience, I fully see her love for me. Not because of the stereo, but because she actually sees how hard I am working as a young man, making it easier for me.

That's the difference between mom and grandma. Grandma will just buy the stereo for me when I mention I want it, whether she can afford it or not. Mom sees my work efforts and takes it from there. She might want to just buy it for me, too, but understands this won't help me grow and learn from the experience. These two ladies are

Chapter 3: Our Lady

my example growing up. What I know and what I love. My two Holy Ladies. I am blessed!

Just like a mom should, she knows my strengths, my weaknesses, my temper (at times), my caring, my trying to make everyone happy, my twenty-year-old naivety, and my selfishness. She knows me after twenty years, feeling a disturbance happening with her child. In an attempt to save me from some future drama with people who don't have my best interest in mind, she says to me one day, "Michael, I think you're getting played by some people who really are all about themselves!"

I know exactly what she means, but I turn a blind eye and a deaf ear to her and the problems I am facing. Walking away, I choose not to see it and not to hear her. Damn pride! Like I have all the answers at twenty. Looks like I'm going to have to learn this all on my own with all the lumps, bruises, anger, and headaches that come with it.

When this conversation goes down, I am in the car backing out of the driveway. She walks up signaling to pull down the window. After the words hit me, I finish backing out into our circle, steering the golden mustang around to head up to street. It's older, but it's still pretty fast. It takes a few seconds, but I hit the gas too hard and squeal the tires. All I do is see her through the rear-view mirror, helpless, growing smaller as I speed up the street further away from my home.

In fact, yes, I do take my lumps. It takes some time, but I do. Mom makes up for this a couple years before she passes. Like she has to, she was only trying to get my attention and help me. After what I accomplish in education and work, she sees me playing on the ground with the twins, like I've done with all my kids. She takes me aside and tells me, smiling, "You know what, you're one of the best fathers I've ever seen!" Through some tough times, I make up for it. She sees it and smiles. I love to see her smile.

The comparison and contrast fully express Our Blessed Mother in what She does for all Her children. God confronts Her with requests a couple times in Her life. Once, when the Angel Gabriel informs Her that the Father requests Her assistance, to be the Mother of His Son, Jesus. Then the second time, at the foot of the cross, Jesus requests His own Mother to be the Mother of all of us. Our Lady says, "YES!" both times.

Jesus takes His Mother to Heaven in the Assumption because of Her impact on the world. Past, present, and future. A Coronation in Heaven takes place. One of the biggest blow outs the entire Universe has ever seen. An event we know happens but are not privy to with our original sin embedded in us and the addiction we have to it. We didn't earn the right to witness Our Lady being Crowned the Queen of Heaven and earth. But the Father allows the results of it for us if we can only embrace Her. Saying, "YES" allows Her to keep Her foot on the serpent, protecting us, and leading us all to Jesus. Eventually, we will share in the Heaven, our choice.

When mom passes, Our Lady takes over and leads me in the right direction. Leading me away from my own selfishness. When I begin praying every day trying to alleviate my burden, I feel like I know Her so well already. Because of mom and grandma, the relationship is there. I don't want to let Her down and see the "worry" look on Her face, like grandma, or experience a quiet spell, like mom either. Our Lady has so many children she is protecting. Protecting Her heart becomes important to me.

Chapter 3: Our Lady

Preceding this way, building Her up, and further examining Her compares to the *Hail Mary*. The prayer begins with the salutation from the Angel Gabriel, *Hail Mary, full of grace, the Lord is with thee.* God's graces shine brightly on His own Mother. *Blessed are You among Women, and Blessed is the Fruit of Thy Womb Jesus.* Elizabeth exuberantly bestows on Mary. She knows exactly what God has in store for Her and Her Son. Finally, Our Lady, becoming Mother to all of us. Her children request with tears, *Holy Mary, Mother of God, Pray for us sinners, Now and at the Hour of our death. Amen.* We ask Her to intercede and pray for us all.

She isn't without tears herself. At the Presentation in the Temple, Simeon foretells of Jesus' suffering and death. The prophecy is piercing Mary's heart with a sword ever since. The agony becoming worse with each passing year as the Passion draws near. Mother Mary experiences this agony over the course of Jesus' life, not just in the course of a couple hours of prayer. Also, with all of us when we turn away.

Mother Mary walks with Jesus when He carries the cross. She sees His suffering. The mockery of the crown of thorns, along with His bruised and bloodied body under the weight of a heavy cross. Mother Mary is right there in the moment, supporting Her Son. There is nothing She can do but let it happen and trust the Father.

Then grabbing Him, squeezing His lifeless body as it is taken down from the cross on Golgotha. Michelangelo's Pieta sculpture represents the scene and Mary's somber face. Real-life showing, Her clothes, hands and face are smeared with His Blood, too, once Hers. The amount of pain She experiences on Good Friday doesn't compare to the prediction of the future so many years before.

As the body of Jesus is pierced by a crown of thorns and nailed to the cross, the sword piercing His Mother lunges further into Her heart. The result of God's children turning away. Proving whatever happens to the Son will also happen to His Mother. There is no line of distinction, only unity here. Mother Mary accepts this, accepting it long ago. Once it becomes reality for Her, pointing out the piety, it comes out as a solemn reverence.

Mother Mary's solemn face portrayed on the Pieta sculpture reminds me of my mom's own solemn face on the night we lost my brother Patrick. No emotion—both are cried out. Many of mom and dad's friends describe how difficult it is to lose an adult child. From giving them hugs and kisses on their pudgy, little faces to guiding them in their formative years up through supporting their successes while growing into what they want to be in life. It's gut wrenching! Just like me and Christopher, mom is always in Patrick's corner, through the good times and bad.

I promise Our Lady my honor and devotion to Her every day. Saying the entire Rosary early every morning begins on December 21, 2020, continuing to this day. She bestows on me many graces keeping me in line with the faith. Sin isn't eliminated but held at bay as long as I regularly go to Confession. She walks alongside me and my family every day. I can't smile until I see My Holy Mother smile along with Her Son, Jesus.

One morning in January 2021 after I say the Rosary and accompanying prayers, I am attentively listening in the dark. I receive a nudge. The nudge is in the form of a question maybe a statement, asking me, "Our Lady is asking about my devotion to Her?!" Right away, I feel a little bit slighted as I am honoring Her. This is a totally

Chapter 3: Our Lady

selfish thought on my part. Then ... I know exactly what She's referring to.

I take for granted that going to Mass and Confession are too time consuming in my busy life, work, family, etc., etc. Especially in the midst of Covid's lockdown. Eventually, it is always taken for granted that we will not be attending. All excuses saying, "I can't go today!" It's just too tough to go." Well, ... I've got plenty of time now.

This is what a mother does for her child. Reminding them of the important things that must be done in life. Not nitpicking but lovingly bringing out what will make her child a better person. A little nudge with the sweet voice of suggestion, getting back on the right track. Not the, "I told you so!" self-righteous tone that we hear so many times in our lives.

I go to Confession that day with Mass afterwards. My last Confession was probably before mom's funeral. Mass, probably Christmas 2020. Since this time, I have faithfully gone to Mass every Sunday and attend all Holy days of obligation. Confession every couple months or so. This is not tooting my horn but is necessary for me to be me. It's the minimum we owe Jesus and His Mother with all Their hard work and suffering put forth for us. The smile on both Their faces is priceless. The happiness in my own heart when I feel this isn't too bad either.

Easter Sunday, April 4, 2021, is the day I officially come back full circle again. Easter Mass allows all of us to be baptized again, not as infants, but as adults. The priest goes around the church, dipping palm leaves into water and splashing it all over us. I get smacked right in the face with water that day. Father chuckles as he goes by. I willingly renew my Baptism and smile, too. "I deserve it Father, Amen!"

A renewal can't happen without a celebration. That's the sacrifice of the Eucharist. As I receive Jesus on this Holy Day, the previous year is replaying in my head. Once I receive Jesus, it stops, I feel Him in me. My Lord and Savior telling me, "Trust in Me and Forgive!" The trust is there building up stronger each day, but the forgiveness will take a while. Definitely both are necessary in order to receive all of God's graces. Still, a tear appears when I kneel down before Him. I will work on both of these requests. This is why I always bring a couple tissues in my pocket to Mass. Just in case.

I see full, vibrant color once more. The way our Father intends for us to see the world. Sin washes away. It all starts with Mother Mary. She takes over, answering all my questions. She leads me back to Her Son again. No doubt about it! She fulfills Her promise to me. It's not just given away and forgotten. We have to work on our faith daily, hourly, by the minute in order to keep it.

This is a huge deal. But the cycle is not completed yet. Yes, Jesus has my attention now. It's Jesus' turn to help me, if I still want it. I still have a "big" area of my life that I need to change. Believe it or not, it's right there in front of me, all of us, with the words within Our *Father*. Are they just words, or do they actually have meaning under Heaven? We will soon see.

Connie's job goes from furlough to reemployment to officially being eliminated in the Spring of 2021. In this moment, I'm still scrounging around for appointments and looking for employment on the outside. The month after we go to Confession and Mass again results in Connie accepting a new position working from home with more money, and me with more appointments. Obviously, we're still

Chapter 3: Our Lady

not rich but now able to at least live paycheck to paycheck with the ability to save some, too.

Think about what just happened. The bottom line is Our Lady loves us very much. With me on the right track again, we are now able to breathe and live without the anxiety every day. True honor and devotion to my Blessed Mother bestows graces and answers all my prayers. Not always what we expect, when we expect it, but the blessings are there on God's time. Fervently saying the Rosary daily, while going to Mass and Confession, regularly all combine to our well-being in this life. We are choosing Heaven and Eternity, putting Jesus and His Mother on a pedestal with emphasis over the disappointments of this world.

Our Lady loves us—that is true. Love and mercy are Heaven. Saying, "YES!" is Her choice, which is the icing on the cake. The exclamation point on love begins with choice. In stark contrast, the evil one's choice is saying, "NO!" Heaven will not allow this, it can't, love and mercy cannot intermix with "NO!

"No, I can't love you. No, I'm too good for you. No, I will not respect you ... I want your soul to prove my point!" The devil says. Like mixing vinegar with bleach, turning into an abrasive chlorine gas. This is why St. Michael and Our Lady are at war with its legions.

After my annulment was officially approved in 2007, Connie and I are married in the Catholic Church. Michaela is four, Caitie is fourteen, and Zach is almost eighteen. This is hard! So much drama combined with situations that just don't need to happen, but they do. When I meet Connie about three years before, I make a promise not to argue anymore, no matter what happens.

It just doesn't matter in the long run. Who cares who wins an argument! Plus no one can argue with a liar and win. When both are liars, ... WATCH OUT! People have a hard time learning this, or their pride takes over and they simply forget.

Just have a nice day. Kind of like I did after being bullied years ago. I don't demand to be right. The best way to maneuver through these stubborn issues is kindness. Sometimes, my kindness is as simple as not talking because so many people just can't handle the truth.

My wife actually makes an effort to do things for my kids. They eventually turn into her kids, too. Connie plans the parties for them, their birthdays, their graduations, their athletic events. Along with coordinating medical appointments, doctor and orthodontist, etc., etc. Paying for them, too. When the kids come over for "my" weekend, it turns into "our" weekend. She is right there to parent, helping me raise them or just sitting by me being my rock.

Money seems to always be at issue. I am very proud of how hard all of my kids work and their understanding of money at such an early age. They support themselves in many cases even though they did have access to ample child support. We do help them a bit with school after high school, a couple cars, and some other items. Not much, but when we do, it is Connie's money. Some we give them, and some they pay back. All agreed to, they don't take advantage of us.

When Michaela decides to live with us full time, she is about fourteen. Connie takes on the same role she does with our three boys – mom. She says, "YES!" in all of these instances. Whether they are her bio kids or her step kids doesn't matter. Let's stop the word play and just say kids.

All examples of a strong woman, reminding me of my own mom and grandma. This is more of the icing on the cake with an exclamation point. Examples of what Our Holy Mother does for us. Connie just does it. I don't have to ask. Along with me seeing grandma Bluvas' faith over the years and my mother-in-law, Connie's mom, with her acceptance of my children, too … I have and have had five "Holy Ladies" here on earth. A total of six. Again, I am very blessed!

St. Joseph is my designated spiritual father. Our Catholic Church refers to him as "The Terror of Demons." in line with our Holy Mother and St. Michael. Another piece of Heaven the evil one must contend with. As a husband to Mother Mary on earth, Father Joseph portrays patience, humility, mercy, chastity, while leaving behind rushing to judgment. The necessary strength to lead the Holy Family to safety into Egypt for a time when Herod proclaims death to all first born males.

Every morning, I thank St. Joseph for guiding me as a young man into fatherhood with his protection. As a father, he has many admirable qualities. These I also pray for … patience, humility, mercy, non-judgment, being less selfish with my time, and the chastity issue. Over the last few years, I definitely have felt better about portraying these qualities. Especially the patience. With a clear head, all of the other qualities seem to fall in line while emotion moves over.

I ask myself when presented with issues, "Does this situation really matter in our Heaven and Eternity?" Most of the time, the answer is no. And I let it go. Examples like driving issues, winning ball games, or what to have for dinner, … etc. All little stuff under Heaven. Using this as a guideline makes "let it go" decisions quite easy. Pride and ego pretty much equal control—don't need them anymore. I trust Jesus … or try to!

Self-control in all of these qualities is another power weapon we have in our arsenal when dealing with the evil one. "Give me the patience to get through hard times, and give me the humility to credit others for great ideas." Releasing control and giving it to Jesus.

I also have to bear the strength to protect my family in today's environment. The turmoil that erupts as this world continually is fighting Heaven. Again, patience and humility. In order to teach my family the importance of our faith and how to handle certain situations, it is necessary to be a loving drill sergeant when disciplining. Like Jesus turning over the tables of corruption in the temple. Keep in mind He only did this once. I don't explode often as long as my children know it's locked up inside me.

Mother Mary and Father Joseph as wife and husband experience the innocence and purity of Heaven here on earth. They are married; they love each other, are good to one another, respect each other, and communicate. The couple always portrays a good role model for Jesus, their families, and their community where they live. Because God asks each of them to bring up His Son, they are in a different state here on earth. They choose this as a piece of Heaven on earth. In a pure love and mercy relationship, there is no need for the physicality of intimate relations.

The Father instills this intimacy for all married couples when a man and a woman commit to one another in the Sacrament of Matrimony here on earth. We as children of God are here to make our spouse better. Better meaning putting Jesus first; the goal is each other's Heaven and Eternity. The gift for being a good wife and a good husband brings each spouse closer to Heaven. The married couple keeps each other grounded in what is actually important by throwing away selfishness. We can get lost at times. But by embracing Mary and Joseph and their Son, Jesus, with the goal being Heaven and Eternity, graces flow in the direction of the married couple.

The Rosary

> How did I get here? It starts with Mother Mary leading me to Her Son. She shows me a better way to count and measure. Counting money isn't that important. That is the Rosary beads I count now, reliving the lives of Jesus and Mary.
>
> **Journal Entry February 2021**

Archbishop Fulton Sheen once commented that saying the Holy Rosary is like yelling out "I love You" to Our Blessed Mother over and over again! She is right there with Her love available, leading us to Jesus. Many Catholics and non-Catholics alike listen to this man in the mid-twentieth century. After watching him on YouTube, I can fully attest that he makes our Faith easy enough for all of us to understand. His Catholic Truth is based on reality, even today.

The drummer is the backbone of a song, keeping the timing, driving the rhythm through the chorus and multiple verses. Holding it together. A true genius on the drums fundamentally keeps the intended beat of the song but takes it further into back-beats or mini-beats. Eventually catching back up to the main beat. More drive, fully blending the other instruments and the singer's voice into the message of the song.

God is so massive that He can be overwhelming to His children. The Holy Spirit is the commanding, intense stage light, highlighting the stage participant and even the audience at just the right time. Mother Mary is that backbone, the drummer holding all of us together. Take the Rosary. When it is said, many *Hail Marys* and *Our Fathers* are prayed over and over again.

Kind of the same process with the guitars. We have a rhythm guitar that is strumming the chords, and the lead guitar striking notes, usually with a bit of a solo towards the end of the song. Further blending it together with all of the instruments and the singer's voice into the message of the song. True musicians at work, sharing their love of music and their messages with all of their audience.

Did I forget the bass guitar. No … the bass is God. This starts the line of succession. The deep, majestic expression of the song. Its foundation is what the entire band takes its cues from. The other instruments play with loving devotion, embellishing the Father's message. The Father is there being stoic and contained. Maybe showing a bit of a mischievous smile at times, having fun with His band. He doesn't need to be animated; everyone understands His power and His place.

Jesus is the frontman. He is smooth, hitting all the necessary notes. His range is phenomenal. Getting the audience into it as the song plays out. The saints and the clergy falling in line. The saints are the orchestra; the clergy and nuns are backup singers. Highlighting their Savior. Father Joseph is the keyboardist set up next to Mother Mary.

Chapter 3: Our Lady

Leaders and laity, we are the gonzo guitarists. Hopefully, going off when needed. We have the choice of staying in line or going rogue with our egos. Remember, Jesus has the microphone, and the Holy Spirit has the light. They can take over at any time.

The band is set up to bring in the audience, reaching all of their senses, ultimately their hearts. The power of the stage light will highlight them, too, at times, as they gravitate closer and closer to the stage. All of them are thirsting for a taste of stardom on God's platform.

Tickets are free, people get in with God-given graces and available sacraments. Use them to get in and be "one of the band" forever. St Michael will allow the closeness and kick out the knuckleheads as necessary. Emulating our heroes, putting ourselves in the party, pretending the musicians are our best friends. When in fact the way I describe it, they are!

Many people have a hang-up and hesitate about saying a prayer repeatedly in one sitting. Maybe that's why this hasn't been voted best band ever … has never been voted into the Rock and Roll Hall of Fame? Kidding aside, I ask this in terms of a favorite song. These songs infuse us with happiness, bringing back memories of both good and bad times in our lives. How many times do we repeat the chorus in these songs? Singing them in our heads. We never hesitate to take part, keeping the words alive within us. It makes us happy, especially if we're feeling down. Singing the same chorus throughout the day in our heads. No hesitancy here, right!

We'll even play "air" guitar, "air" drums, or sing into an "air" microphone when we hear our favorite songs. We do this over and over again. Think of an eternity of playing "air" notes. "Man, I love this song!" How many times throughout our lives have we done this? Isn't it repetitive, and loving life? Should we stop? Hey, I even play bongos on the table next to me once in a while. In my head I'm a professional.

Now we belong when we genuinely join this band. There's plenty of room. We don't have to play "air" notes our entire life! This is the basis for our Catholic Faith, highlighting the song played with the Holy Rosary. Divided into five decades. Each decade associated with one of the events of the daily Mystery from Mother Mary's and Jesus' lives. The repetition when said from the heart with true meaning forces the evil one off its game. Throw in the life event described in the Mystery, meditating on it, and evil has a serious issue. No choice but to slither away and regroup. Doing it daily, Mother Mary keeps Her foot on the serpent's head. Giving us the firepower of gatling gun canons that don't miss.

Back in high school when I say my first full Rosary, this profound meaning didn't exist in my head. Unfortunately, I didn't know about it, so it becomes boring with no focus. I hadn't developed a true relationship with Our Lady yet. I wasn't aware of this even during my Holy Hour of Adoration back about twenty-five years ago either. To a degree I follow my picture prayer card, each colorful picture catches my eye. But it doesn't fully click with what I'm doing at the time. No relationship yet. It takes my "fiery ordeal" for it to fully click.

Now when I say the Rosary, I feel the rhythm of the prayer, then the beat takes over. Now, I hear everything. The drive is my love for Mother Mary, leading me to Her Son. The mini-beats within the main beat are the Mysteries. The single notes of the guitar are the events within each Mystery. Reflecting on the events of the Mystery

Chapter 3: Our Lady

with each respective bead fully blends the masterpiece together. The blending is a beautiful song of love for Our Blessed Mother, leading us to Her Son, Jesus. The perfect song sang over and over again. All because I have developed a relationship with my Mother Mary.

Remember I mentioned Elvis Presley back in chapter one. To me, this is "The King … of rock and roll" and part of my heaven on earth with grandma and grandpa. This guy is my idol even today. I realize he was a humble man, sharing his wealth with many. Elvis loved his mother, and our Father in Heaven, thinking of all the religious songs he recorded. Good guys have bad days and tempers can flare. I'm no different, I've put my fist through walls before, too. I also understand wanting to deaden the pain we all carry with us during hard times. He deserved a lot more from some of his own people he loved and idolized. And to another extent, vice versa.

Evil is slithering about in the world. I definitely can relate and have many more good days than bad. Why do I mention this? Because he recorded a song called *"The Miracle of the Rosary"* on the *Elvis Now* album in 1972.

Father's Day, June 19th, 1977, my mom and dad take Pat and me to see Elvis in Omaha. They learn their lesson when I have a meltdown in 1974, when I didn't get a ticket to go. It was one of his last concerts. People are still amazed I remember the date. When he passes a few months later, many of his albums are available again in the record stores. I choose albums based on how cool he looks on the cover. *Elvis Now* was one of the albums my grandma bought for me.

My mom and grandma love *"The Miracle of the Rosary"* as we play it over and over again on the big console stereo in the living room. Great memories of this song making them happy. I still have this song slotted in on many of my playlists. That's what I know.

What I learn from *Fr. Donald Calloway* and his terrific book written in 2016, *Champions of the Rosary: The History and Heroes of a Spiritual Weapon,* published by Marian Press, is a wealth of information about the history of the Rosary. Some of what I already know from Catholic school, but still a lot of the details in this book are new to me. After reading it, I'm able to put it all together. From St. Dominic through to today.

On page 167, Fr. Calloway mentions this song, *"The Miracle of the Rosary"* by Elvis. It comes out about the same time both St. Pope Paul VI and the bishops in the United States are proposing ways to "renew interest in the Rosary" for their flocks after Vatican II—a very important aim from the conference about eight years earlier.

Fr. Calloway has his own story about Sanctity and Mercy. How he got there with his book, *No Turning Back – A Witness to Mercy.* Read about his transformation. Take note of how pictures of him throughout the years tell the story. Focus on his eyes and the lost stare. He is devoted to Our Lady. Our Mother led him back to Jesus!

To this day Elvis Presley is the only major recording artist releasing a song about the Rosary in 1972. The song, *"Miracle of the Rosary,"* is written by a childhood friend, Lee Denson. It comes out at a time when Mother Mary needs it. After Vatican II, our world needs it. One of the aims is to show honor and devotion to Our Lady by promoting the Rosary. I like to believe the release of this song provides a tremendous boost to this effort. Elvis wasn't Catholic, but it is interesting how he was always thirsting for the Truth. Even though he is a well-known entertainer.

Chapter 3: Our Lady

Elvis Presley also records another religious song in the same recording session called, *"The Lord's Prayer."* It is more of an informal recording never winding up on an actual album of the period, only later on with all of his religious recordings. Christians attest to this prayer as it starts and ends with Our Father in Heaven. It has been recorded by a select few other artists as well. This is another indirect shot, telling the evil one to stay away. More gatling guns a blazing in my Heaven on earth.

Since we're talking music in this section, let's continue with Dion DiMucci, better known as Dion, who is part of that same past I take refuge in when growing up. I love his older music along with his newer stuff, it's all pure, raw … music. Just like Elvis, this takes me to places where I can be me, with my grandparents. Singing this stuff over and over again in my head and playing these songs in my playlists.

I mention Dion because I've followed him throughout the years. Another world-wide entertainer bearing the cross of Jesus. Like all of us, he has had his demons. And Dion conquers them with the help of his wife and the Holy Spirit. He has done many interviews on *EWTN*, promoting his Catholic Faith. I am amazed. I recently listened to, *"Dion: The Rock and Roll Philosopher"* his latest book. All I can say is it's terrific. Again, Our Mother is constantly leading Her children back to Jesus.

Dion defines his truth more specifically in his book, *Dion: The Wanderer Talks Truth* from 2011. His Truth is his Catholic Faith that he comes back to. Now fully understanding it, spreading it like Peter and Paul. Many scripture passages accompany this Truth. It is a well-written description of Catholicism transparent enough for anyone struggling with their own faith. Along with Mike Aquilina, Dion relates his struggles and successes in his life. According to Dion today, success is his family and his faith. Another great template for people struggling with their faith to follow.

Then there's Dean Martin. Italian yes, Catholic maybe? But he grew up that way. One day I pull up a song he recorded in the 1960's on YouTube. The song is entitled, *"In The Misty Moonlight"* written by Cindy Walker. It is so innocent about being with your girlfriend or boyfriend that it brings tears to my eyes. The melody is innocent, Dino's voice is true, well ... it's Dean Martin! This captures my Heaven on earth with grandma and grandpa.

After this, I bring up a Dion and The Belmonts tune recorded in 1960, *"Where or When."* Then, I catch a couple Elvis movies. *"Blue Hawaii"* and *"Follow That Dream."* Pure innocence. Although they are not alive at this time, I understand the difference between music and culture then to now.

I'm an old soul. Might be a bit of a "nerd," but I always pretend I'm Elvis in these movies, romancing the girl, singing the song, *"Can't Help Falling In Love,"* then living happily ever-after with the girl I love. Even as a little boy of seven or eight – my Heaven on Earth with grandma and grandpa. I push this dream a bit early on in my life. I experience the reality of making decisions and suffering the consequences of not living happily ever after. But God has since granted this blessing to me.

I also catch another YouTube video of Dean Martin coming out of a Los Angeles restaurant in his older years. He looks older than we remember but still had fire in the belly wanting to talk with people. Then I think ... think of all his stories, his knowledge and experiences that were lost with his passing. It would have been a great privilege to be able to go back into that restaurant and listen to him talk! Wow!

Same with Dion, who is still alive and kicking. And ultimately, Elvis. Again, wow! Just sitting there and talking with them like one of the guys in the barbershop or the beer joint (there's a word for you, bar today). Taking in their stories, just listening, respecting them.

I would also give anything to sit down and listen to my two grandpas. Again, wow! To a degree I listened when they were still with us, but not with the respect that is owed them. To make up for it all, I listen, honor, and respect my own dad ... Mother Mary and Father Joseph.

There is an innocence, a purity, and a respect in saying the Holy Rosary that's always there if we can just pick one up and say it. That's my point. Innocence has been lost in our music, culture, and families. People in the spotlight today aren't necessarily the most talented, but they do bring in their own unique edge. That edge grows edgier and more degrading to humanity. Now just about anyone can join in with easy social media access. Everyone can have their own minute of fame. Saying the Rosary will always keep this innocence and purity in our daily lives. Embrace it forever, and these will never leave you.

I believe America's innocence was lost on November 22nd, 1963, with the assassination of our president, John F. Kennedy. And his words, "Ask not what your country can do for you – ask what you can do for your country," went with him. Further proven with what happened to Martin Luther King Jr. in 1968. Evil and its group pounce on us when we don't say the Rosary!

Oh, my Jesus, forgive us our sins, save us from the fires of hell, lead all souls to Heaven, especially those in most need of your mercy.

The Fatima Prayer, Mother Mary to the 3 children at Fatima

I don't have an outside sprinkler system dug into my lawn. Instead, I use old fashioned sprinklers attached to a long hose, reaching both my front and back yards. Each time I cut the grass, I have to roll up the long hose—ideally rolling it up into a circle so it doesn't knot like a cowboy rope. Easy enough the first time the grass is watered.

As the summer progresses and gets hotter discipline evades me; I end up throwing the hose on the side of the house off the grass. Towards fall, so many knots have taken hold that it takes a miracle for me to untie them all. I do it to myself. Every year, I promise myself, "Next year, I will roll up the hose like I should … or, bite the bullet and put in a sprinkler system!?"

The twenty-first century so ties this world into knot-after-knot, I lose count. We are getting so technologically savvy, we tell ourselves, "Hey, God, thanks for your efforts, but I think we got it now!" We've pushed aside the First Commandment, "I am the Lord Your God, You shall have no other gods before Me!" With this mentality, emotion takes over. Patience is lost. Order is lost to clutter. How many horrific wars are fought? Where's the humility? Wealth and prestige become the definition of success and gods onto themselves. We need our Mother!

Fatima. For six months in 1917 *"Our Lady of the Rosary"* appears to three little children, Lucia, Francisco, and Jacinta, in Portugal tending their sheep. My Fatima pamphlet mentioned in Chapter 1

Chapter 3: Our Lady

leads me to say the full Rosary for the first time. It is hard. I am bored. Instead, I am lost to this world. A full understanding of the true Rosary is lost on me until God's fire during the pandemic of Covid-19. Although hidden, the message stays with me. It doesn't fully manifest itself into a full flame of loving devotion to Our Lady for almost forty years.

There is so much more to this vision of Mother Mary. Forty years is a long time in people years. I place me and my own made-up world first. Ahead of God. Thinking I will eventually back into God as I live my life. Instead of going straight to His graces and love, I take a number of turns, pivoting around like a rat in a maze. I can smell the cheese; it's only a trap though. I can't find my way out of it. My own selfishness takes some effort. These efforts fail me.

The three Fatima children realize God comes first with the help of Mother Mary. At a young age, they yearn for God by seeing the beauty of our Holy Mother, face-to-face, smiling at them in person from Heaven. They also live with actually seeing Her sad face in tears with Her heart surrounded by the thorns of all of our sins. Then the children see a vision of hell. Its flames engulfing eternal sinners with their devils. All a profound and loving gift to the three little children from their Holy Mother.

How do they go back to their lives after having this stamped into their heads? Ok, back to life as normal? No, they pray more often, more vibrantly, saying the Rosary, and making sacrifices. They pray with meaning from their hearts. This allows their Holy Mother to smile, making "Her" happy, lessening "Her" pain. Doing it all for Her and the world as She requests. When people place God first in their lives, they don't end up waiting around and wallowing about in this world. They are driven to do God's Will.

Mother Mary's appearance and words from Fatima take on an even greater meaning today. The years 1917 and 2020 … through to 2025, are remarkably similar times. In 1917, Mother Mary requests that the little children tell the world to devotedly pray and say the Rosary to stop wars and wickedness … in particular pray for the Consecration of Russia to the Holy Mother as requested in later years.

October 13, 1917, is the last vision. Thousands of onlookers see "The Miracle of the Sun" play out, promoting Mother Mary's promise of a miracle for people to believe She is actually there in Portugal. For a few moments, the sun dances around in glorious colors, zigging and zagging, coming close to the earth on its crazy trajectory. Then suddenly veering off. This craziness dries up the dark, miserable, rainy conditions on that day. When the sun goes back into place, the day is bright, everyone and everything is dry once more.

To an extent Mother Mary intercedes, keeping Her promise, doing what She can for us. Obviously, during this time there is a resurgence of God's children picking up their Rosaries and praying enough for this to occur. World War I ends about a year later in 1918.

But the reality of Mother Mary actually appearing from Heaven subsides into distant memory for many, not all, but many in just a few years. A worse war with many more deaths, World War II begins in 1939. There is a clear drop-off in saying the Rosary. Afterwards, Soviet Russia sets up its empire, eating up the free world—showing everyone that we can't stop and remain lax in our devotion for a minute.

Chapter 3: Our Lady

Remember when I state in Chapter 1, referring to 2020 and my journaling, "This confusing time has the earth encircling the sun in erratic fashion, causing my head to spin right along with it." Sure craziness. I contend here that the earth is the object moving around in an erratic trajectory infused by craziness because of politics and people's bad decisions. Order and law become just words. Whatever it is, I'm dizzy. But I feel God working. I need to pray and say the Rosary, too, just like everyone at that time. Each generation must learn, stepping up to the challenge. The miracle here is mine that I must share, just like Peter and Paul are the first generation getting out the Truth of the Gospels.

Both time periods experience world-wide flu-pandemics a century apart. Many people die in each of them. Little Francisco and Jacinta catch the illness and pass away. Both are made saints because they put God first and take on Mother Mary's requests with no hesitation in prayer, sacrifice, or suffering.

Lucia becomes Sr. Lucia and lives a long life in a convent with a cloistered environment. She writes her memoirs documenting her experiences in Fatima with her little cousins. Mother Mary and Jesus visit her a couple more times throughout her life as she has more to fulfill. She is given more secrets and vows silence until Mother Mary designates the right time to be revealed. One is the Consecration of Russia to Our Holy Mother must be made in order to save the world from the errors of Russia, understood to be atheistic communism, spreading throughout the world. And, two is a vision of the future, showing Catholic laity, clergy, and bishops lying bloodied on the ground, lifeless. Representing the persecutions of those who believe.

Karol Wojtyla from Poland bridges the early twentieth century and Fatima into its later years. Connecting what Mother Mary requests with the reality of fulfillment. This man is better known as Saint Pope John Paul II, becoming pope in 1978. All of the wars and communism prove evil, and its legions are here on earth slithering about. They keep tying their selves around the earth. Each year, the knots increase, becoming tighter.

Karol is a big supporter of Our Blessed Mother and the Rosary. His own mother passes early on in his life; he never really knows her. In this instance, Mother Mary steps in as his mother here on earth, too. He is devoted to Her throughout his entire life. This is the relationship Karol Wojtyla knows.

Mother Mary knows Her child, too. She recognizes his cries, his needs, his wants, his worries, his happiness, developing him into a future pope. She follows God's will. Through the Nazi invasion of Poland, keeping him safe in his prayer group meetings and when performing plays, both outlawed at the time. She keeps Poland's Catholic religion and culture sacred and hidden from destruction by these despots.

Unfortunately, these have to stay hidden with the defeat of the Nazis right on through to the end of the Soviet Union in 1991. More than fifty years, half a century, plus. Tyrannical governments, from fascists to communists. Both oppressors, not much of a difference when igniting the same evil.

PJP II speaks out against communism and all of its lies and deceptions. This man can attest because he lives through it all, understanding the evil coming with these tyrants. It affects him, his faith, his country, and the world. Both push his Mother Mary away with

Chapter 3: Our Lady

Her Son and prohibit God's children from knowing their own unique dignified individuality. No modern fact-check is necessary. Pope John Paul II is God's fact-check.

Vatican II is the support underneath necessary for the connecting bridge between Fatima and PCP II. He begins finalizing the aims of the Catholic Church from Vatican II. One of those aims, a very important one, is sticking up for his Mother, fighting for Her. The Mother he knows.

PCP II is promoting more devotion and honor to Mother Mary. And, also, St Joseph, because of his own devotion and humility shown toward his Spouse. Both members of the Holy Family, nurturing the young Jesus here on earth. Honor and devotion are a must in prayers and good works offered to them. He knows continually saying the Holy Rosary with devotion from the heart is necessary to retain peace and salvation in the world.

Mother Mary and Her Son, Jesus, are one. She suffers and He suffers because of our decisions. Our Lady will always lead Her children to Jesus. Just as She does with her son, PCP II. Father Joseph always protects us whenever we request it. Like he does when the Holy Family flees for safety in Egypt.

Three years into his papacy, on May 13, 1981, Pope John Paul II survives an assassination attempt. Two bullets hit him while out amongst the people, smiling and waving. One is almost lethal. The crowd sees his blood stained white cloak, leaving his life in question until doctors quickly get to him at the hospital. Mother Mary prevents his death, saves Her son, because of his devotion and love toward Her throughout his life. On December 27, 1983, he meets the shooter, Mehmet Ali Ağca, in Rome's Rebibbia Prison, publicly forgiving him. This event is turned into a "piece of Heaven here on earth" moment because of Our Lady and Her son Saint Pope John Paul II.

Think of the evil that is conjured up making this happen. The hate taking over the shooter and the group he runs with, filling all of Satan's followers with their own type of back-assed joy. PJP II bluntly stops it. The serpent stops, backs up, and slithers away. Just as *"The Our Father"* requests us to do when someone wrongs us. Forgiveness is power God gives to all of us.

Pope John Paul II meets with Sr Lucia early on in his papacy. One of the last items Our Lady of Fatima requests is consecrating Russia to Her on a world-wide basis for all to hear. The entire world, including the complete entourage of Church Cardinals and Bishops. After Mass in St. Peter's Square on March 25, 1984, PCP II kneels down before the Blessed Mother, performing the ceremony that will fully Consecrate Russia to Her.

Sr. Lucia confirms, "The Consecration is accepted by Heaven." It is complete as Our Mother requests. We know that God's time is not ours. The Berlin Wall falls in late 1989, and there is a peaceful implosion of the Soviet Union in 1991. Communism in Europe is no more. This is Our Mother's Promise after Her request is finally fulfilled. She intercedes for Her children once again.

Saint Pope John Paul II also added the *Luminous Mysteries* to the Holy Rosary of Our Mother. This provides a total of four Mysteries to dwell on and think about when praying the Rosary. These are said on Thursdays. They are (1) *The Baptism of Jesus*, (2) *The Wedding Feast at Cana*, (3) *Heaven is Revealed*, (4) *The Transfiguration*, and (5) *Jesus Gives Us the Eucharist*.

To be clear, here are the *Three Mysteries* we have already attached to the Holy Rosary.

The *Joyous Mysteries* are said on Mondays and Saturdays. They are (1) *The Annunciation,* (2) *The Visitation,* (3) *The Birth of Jesus,* (4) *The Presentation in the Temple,* and (5) *Finding the Child Jesus in the Temple.*

The *Sorrowful Mysteries* are said on Tuesdays and Fridays. They are (1) *Agony in the Garden,* (2) *The Scourging at the Pillar,* (3) *The Crowning with Thorns,* (4) *Jesus Carries His Cross to Calvary,* and (5) *The Crucifixion and Death of Jesus.*

The *Glorious Mysteries* are said on Wednesdays and Sundays. They are (1) *The Resurrection,* (2) *The Ascension into Heaven,* (3) *The Decent of the Holy Spirit,* (4) *The Assumption of Our Blessed Mother,* and (5) *The Coronation of Our Blessed Mother, Crowned Queen of Heaven.*

The Mysteries are all perfect accompaniments to the Holy Rosary. Here we dwell on these with each of the five decades. Doing this brings out more reverence from our hearts as we say the words with meaning. Well-deserved Honor and devotion to Our Lady. Look at the related Bible verses. We are reading the Bible, too.

We will always have evil within the world; we all know this. This ends one segment of evil that had been chewing up the world since the Russian Revolution in 1917. Horrific wars were fought since then but in this instance communism in Europe was solved peacefully. This could have meant World War III and the destruction of the world as we know it. Instead, it is solved by Our Mother's Intercession. I will say it again … peacefully! All by saying the Rosary with devotion. That's all we have to do. So many other problems could also be solved and avoided. Each year, we need more prayers, more beads counted as more Rosaries are said, keeping up with evil.

Every morning, I say the Holy Rosary I pray for Our Lady's intercession in making Sr. Lucia and Archbishop Fulton Sheen saints! They need to be made saints. Both have been a major influence on the Catholic Church during the twentieth century. Along with Saint Pope John Paul II, who was made a saint in 2014 by Pope Francis. All three in the mix of Our Lady's apparitions as they relate to Our Father's plans. These are strident and obedient souls, honoring Our Lady.

Yes, Vatican II can be considered the support between Fatima and Pope John Paul II, who passed in 2005. An argument can also be made for a pillar of that support being Fulton Sheen. His speeches, books, and TV appearances during mid-twentieth century America are big. I asked my dad if he remembers seeing the Archbishop on TV in the 50's and 60's. He said, "Oh yeah, we'd watch him every week as a family." He was a big deal if dad remembers him with an, "Oh yeah!"

My experience with Fulton Sheen is watching many YouTube videos from when he was on TV. I've also read quite a few of his books. From our Catholic Faith to many on Mother Mary. His take on communism, an atheism taking away our freedom and our souls from God, is a must watch and/or read given the opportunity. He is able to relate our Catholic Faith in an easy to understand voice. Step by step on a subject all easily understood. He had the charisma necessary at the time when TV was new to our country, speaking to his audience not at them. Not damning them all to hell!

Chapter 3: Our Lady

Francisco and Jacinta pass early on after the Fatima apparitions. Sr Lucia still had more to do while bringing out more on Fatima and Our Lady's requests. Since she lived to a ripe old age of ninety-seven, just missing her ninety-eighth birthday in 2005, she had the opportunity to say many Rosaries in her cloistered convent. Interesting how Pope John Paul II and Sr. Lucia passed in the same year, only a few months apart.

Devotion and Promises

I have my collection of Rosaries, medals, and prayer cards blessed by my priest after Confession. This includes all of my "Miraculous Medals" replicas that Mother Mary gave to St Catherine in 1830. I have a bulk of these medals. My intention has always been to place one in the homes, rooms, cars, or even the chairs of people I love.

Journal Entry March 2021

Devotion to Our Blessed Mother should just happen. Unfortunately, our humanness, along with our worldliness, isn't always trusting right away. It takes time for the building of a relationship. This is the reason for Her existence. Because we are scared and frightened of the world we are embracing. Sometimes, we don't have the examples of a mother here on earth as a template. She will lead us away from this world to embrace Jesus instead.

God has created so many avenues where we can embrace our Mother Mary. One of them is the "Miraculous Medal" given to Saint

Catherine of Laboure in 1830 by Our Lady. Just as its name implies, anyone embracing Mother Mary with honor and loving devotion will receive what they ask for. Our Lady's intercession is always there for us, She is God's Mother.

I find another religious pamphlet during my short-lived Holy Hour of Adoration almost thirty years ago now. Like the Fatima pamphlet, I take this message to heart as well. I believe but keep it locked up inside of me. Here, Our Lady appears to Saint Catherine. She is called upon to spread the medal but be obedient in silence. Never mentioning this event until close to her death. Just think of keeping this marvelous news to yourself, except your confessor, for one's whole life.

The medal shows Mother Mary standing on top of the serpent with Her open hands at Her sides. Graces are flowing out onto the world. The message around the medal states, *"O Mary Conceived Without Sin Pray For Us Who Have Recourse To Thee!"* The back side shows twelve stars on the outside with an "M" for Mary under a cross. This signifies the closeness between Mother and Son, with two hearts pierced by all of our sins. Thorns for Jesus and a sword for His Mother as they both share in the suffering.

Interesting how Our Mother appears again in 1858 to Saint Bernadette in Lourdes. Both apparitions occur in France, which is still in uproar since the French Revolution and Napoleon. Over fifty years. Lourdes confirms the message stamped on the medal. Our Lady is "The Immaculate Conception" as the Church has been promoting since 1854. It is proven dogma from Heaven!

These apparitions both transition God's children to the twentieth century and Fatima. Showing mercy, giving us a fighting chance with

Chapter 3: Our Lady

Mother Mary's intercession. Even though it's roughly two hundred years, it's a quick turnaround in God time.

I have to believe these apparitions are the work of Our Lady. She loves us all so much She asks Our Father for more time, more mercy. Just like my mom did for me with my stereo. Don't get me wrong, obviously not even close to the same scale. Not saying that! I'm only stressing their love and how important it is in any circumstance.

Over time, I accumulate many of these medals with the intent of giving them out. But more importantly using them to bring in all my family and friends to Mother Mary, hiding them in their homes or on their person. These are also kept in a tub on a bookshelf by my Bible and Rosaries. I forget about them, too, and let them accumulate dust.

Everyone likes medals. These medals from Heaven are perfect to give out to anyone. I'm starting with family and friends. I've made them into necklaces for the boys, who graciously take them after I discuss the significance of the medal. I even place a medal on my pocket Rosary, carrying it everywhere I go.

I challenge my wife, all of my children, family, friends, and even people at the office to find the "Miraculous Medals" that I have placed in their midst. Right under their noses, close to them. I have fifty plus medals. They are there hidden in between tables, desks, chairs, beds, car dashboards, under sinks, cabinets, junk drawers, … by the toothpaste!? Everywhere and anywhere is fair game. Every morning, I pray they all embrace Our Lady, who will lead them to Her Son Jesus. A good fire has been started. Once found, let's have a discussion and change our Heaven and Eternity goals. In the meantime, I will be living by example. Or attempting to.

The last two hundred years define my devotion to Our Lady. We are in some very progressive times. Moving fast. I'm trying to do my part in order for a solid peace in this world. Now we have issues with Russia and its former Soviet satellite Ukraine. Conflicts aren't only in Europe anymore. They're large scale all over the world. Including these pesky things called bigotry and terrorism. How many people must be subjugated to all of this? ... Pray the Rosary with reverence. Let's get started. Help Our Mother's intercession in the world. Get beaded up now!

Translating the prayers of the Holy Rosary into Latin is very beautiful. Latin is old and mystical just like our Catholic Church. When praying in Latin, or attempting to, I feel I am praying with all of the monks of yester-year that inhabited the monasteries, all of our Popes, and Saints, Benedict and Thomas Aquinas just to name a few. It is an old and established language that the evil one doesn't like. Evil has discredited it. My hope is to always keep it off-guard by using it once in a while.

Hail Mary in Latin

Ave Maria, gratia plena, Dominus tecum; benedicta tu in mulieribus, et benedictus fructus ventris tui, Jesus.

Sancta Maria, Mater Dei, ora pro nobis peccatoribus, nunc et in hora mortis nostrae. Amen.

Catholic Online

Just like Spanish. With so many people speaking various versions of it, I try to learn the Rosary in Spanish, too. Praying right along with our Spanish speaking brothers and sisters. Thanks to Saint Juan Diego, our American southern hemisphere is full of believers. Happening when Our Lady of Guadalupe appears before him from Heaven. Millions of conversions take place in 1531, which is why there are so many Catholics south of the American border. It is the work of Our Lady.

This is big for our hemisphere. Mother Mary is praying for us, Intercessor for all of us. We all must assimilate with each other. We are all connected, interwoven by Her love and our Faith. I pray for law and order, in other words justice. And I pray for a reasonable, not an emotional, path to amnesty and citizenship for all hard-working people inside this country. Removing politics and any group taking advantage of what people are experiencing here. Praying the Hail Mary in Spanish proves I mean business.

Hail Mary in Spanish

Dios te salve, Maria, llena eres de gracia, El Senor es contigo, bendita tu eres entre todas las mujeres, y bendito es el fruto de tu vientre, Jesus.

Santa Maria, Madre de Dios, ruega por nosotros pecadores, ahora y en la hora nuestra muerte. Amen.

Catholic Online

These special languages allow us to work harder in our reverence to Our Lady. I don't know the languages, so it will take longer to say a full Rosary. Two of my great-grandfathers are Lithuanian. One is Czech. Plus there is a bit of German and Irish in me, too. I would love to learn the *Hail Mary* and *Our Father* in all of these languages.

Mother Mary gives the Holy Rosary to Saint Dominic in 1208. There had been various prayers in Her name regarding the highlights of Her and Jesus' lives. Now, all of these culminating in the beads we know today. Dominic also received fifteen Promises that those who pray the Rosary will receive. Embracing Our Lady is a must. So, She can lead those to Jesus. Saying it with the honor, devotion, and reverence She deserves. I want to see Her smile.

1. Whoever shall faithfully serve me by the recitation of the Rosary shall receive signal graces.
2. I promise my special protection and the greatest graces to all those who shall recite the Rosary.
3. The Rosary shall be a powerful armor against hell; it will destroy vice, decrease sin, and defeat heresies.
4. It will cause virtue and good works to flourish ... Oh, that souls would sanctify themselves by this means.
5. The soul which recommends itself to me by the recitation of the Rosary shall not perish.
6. Whoever shall recite the Rosary devoutly shall never be conquered by misfortune.
7. Whoever shall have a true devotion for the Rosary shall not die without the sacraments of the Church.

Chapter 3: Our Lady

8. Those who are faithful to recite the Rosary shall have, during their life and at their death, the light of God.
9. I shall deliver from purgatory those who have been devoted to the Rosary.
10. The faithful children of the Rosary shall merit a high degree of glory in Heaven.
11. You shall obtain all you ask of me by the recitation of the Rosary.
12. All those who propagate the Holy Rosary shall be aided by me in their necessities.
13. All the advocates of the Rosary shall have for intercessors the entire celestial court during their life and at the hour of death.
14. All who recite the Rosary are my sons, and brothers of my only Son Jesus Christ.
15. Devotion of my Rosary is a great sign of predestination.

The Holy Mother Herself to Saint Dominic and Fr. Alan in 1208

I find these on the internet. I use these as a backdrop wallpapering the home screen on my computer and cell phone. It is a beautiful tan background with Mother Mary smiling in the center. These promises make the Rosary a weapon against evil. Mother Mary is pleading with us to devoutly say it as much as possible. As proven by Her apparitions over the last two hundred years. Her message is, "It works!"

Since I've started my routine in the mornings, I have felt so much well-being in life. I am back to being a thriving child of God out of the fire of Covid. Burning with love for everything Heaven allows. My patience has increased, allowing me a clear head to make decisions and handle everyday life and any obstacle that comes my way. And I attempt not to judge without truth.

These promises mean more when you actually embrace Our Lady. Because your goal changes from this world to Heaven and Eternity. When your goal is something in this world, these promises don't mean as much. People will only gloss them over, not acknowledging Heaven, until they really need help.

When embracing Our Lady, these promises become sacred. I can't read them without shedding a tear or two. Because I honor Her by saying the Rosary every day. Based on our relationship, I trust Her; these will all occur. As long as I keep Her high on a pedestal of honor and devotion.

Up to this point, I have been shown the safety net Our Lady provides. All of the Promises and Her love and support will never fade. We as sinners have bad days where the evil one will convince us otherwise. Think of a trapeze artist, practicing over and over again. With all the passion and practice she exhibits, her performance should be perfect. She isn't. Eventually, the performance won't go as planned. Whether she's a few seconds off on a trajectory or she just loses her grip. It'll happen; no one is perfect. Instead of the beautiful lady falling to the ground with a splat and a lifeless body, she is captured within the safety net.

The "fiery ordeal" burns me. Sometimes, the flames become so intense as they engulf my body it feels hopeless. The pain can be unbearable at times. Life and the world get in the way again. In my case, it comes down to money and enduring the lack thereof. I take the easy path and blame God. Yes, after all His graces, I initiate a rebellion. It's not just blame … it's ANGER!

I relapse again, falling off the wagon with a thud. Now the serpent has an opening, and the trap is set. Anger begets all of the loathing I keep within me. The searing red flames of a brain on hate shows me, the bullies, the media, the politicians that take my money, the lockdowns, my child support, the two-faced business partners, my bosses that let me go, … and that double-masked old lady.

"If it wasn't for any of this," I tell myself, "I wouldn't be in this position." It's that simple. No, it's not. I can't take anymore, and my fist goes through a wall with a right-hook. Not enough—I don't feel any better. Then a left-hook. I've never demolished a wall one right after the other in the moment. Now, I hurt worse than I did before.

Chapter 4

REKINDLING THE FIRE

And Jesus entered the temple of God and drove out all who sold and bought in the temple, and he overturned the tables of the money-changers and the seats of those who sold pigeons. He said to them, "It is written, 'My house shall be called a house of prayer'; but you make it a den of robbers."

Matthew 21:12-13

Tables of Corruption

I define myself as being a Blessed Child of God. My greatest achievement is the effort and love I put forth for my wife and children, and grandchild. This is my true happiness, God's gift. Getting them to a good place, faith in God is the goal. Things change dramatically when your goal becomes Heaven and Eternity. I am a temple, corrupt at times, with my family and friends. When the temple is lost, take it back!

Journal Entry March 2024

Red embers hidden within me are shaken up. I feel it. Him working on the scorched me fanning the flame. I have nothing left to offer this world; it has all of my possessions. The world isn't a friend to me.

It has "canceled" me a number of times because I chose it. I chose to get ahead like many others.

When you are given a choice and take a particular path, beware of the consequences. Jesus will show you the "real" consequences of your actions. In a world full of more opportunity than ever before for individuals, the world will only call you a victim of wealthy tyrants, then coddle you, so you become more like them again. They're attempting their own rekindling.

Being "canceled" along with a couple *"George Bailey"* moments lead me to a new conclusion … my goal isn't wealth, prestige, or a house on the lake. I'm already a millionaire with a beautiful wife, six kids, and grandchildren … family and friends on top of this. No, my goal becomes what to do with my soul? My body is growing older; that's only a fact. It's my soul and how it fits in with Heaven and Eternity that matter.

A fiery, hard fact that most people must learn. God's power and time is eternity; we only have a blip in that time to make it right. The point is, "We have the power!" We've all got to get there. Help Jesus overturn the tables of corruption. Follow His lead! Let it ride … bet on Jesus!

"Jesus cleanses the Temple." Matthew sets the scene. More is hiding below the surface than what transgresses. Jesus knows His time on earth is short. We are all late in the game. He has performed miracles that no one can deny except the power brokers of the time. I'm sure these men of politics receive their "fair" share of taxes with another day of commerce in the Temple. He preaches parables mixing in short stories about how our Father wants us to act in order to

Chapter 4: Rekindling the Fire

receive eternal life in Heaven. All emphasizing love and mercy. And He shows us all by example from a simplistic life.

This time Jesus goes berserk, proving God is in His human form. Yelling at all of us, turning over tables, lashing out with His cord as animals escape, money and commerce spill, covering the floor. This is Jesus, giving us all a pep talk as our coach. Pumping us up. We as humans are a mess. Just as the Temple turns into a mess, both spiritually and literally, by His outburst. Jesus will love us all up again when He takes up the Cross, suffering and ultimately dying for all of us on Good Friday. Here, He cleanses the temple of our souls.

Exactly what I need to get back in line with my new goal from the end of the last chapter. Straight talk. Good old-fashioned straight talk from Jesus. Reminding me the urgency of my situation, because we aren't promised tomorrow. I learn more discipline, patience, and humility when taking advantage of our safety net. It's ongoing, realizing I need to learn more.

When we grasp the light of finding Jesus again, it is considered a high point in our lives. I thought I was done and ready for Heaven. There lies the problem … we're not done. It'll happen over and over. Read the Bible and all of the highs and lows of God's children in the Old Testament. We must always be mindful of what Our Mother does for us. Love Her and keep Her on that pedestal as I mention before we were so rudely interrupted by my temper tantrum.

The discipline and patience show me to keep saying the *Hail Mary* and the Holy Rosary. Just say them, and the well-being eventually captures me again. The serpent will leave, and Jesus will take over with the discipline of heartfelt prayer and reverence. I learn to change anger into prayer as I offer it up to Jesus.

I consider myself a loving drill sergeant, too. My job is to make good men and women out of my children, all walking with Jesus. Living by example like St. Joseph isn't always exhibited, but there is always love and discipline shown. At times, especially with my youngest twin, I have to yell and go ape crazy on them. It is the only way they will listen after mentioning an important issue a couple, three, maybe four times with no acknowledgement. This doesn't turn out too well for them, for anyone for that matter.

Since I don't do this all the time, it becomes a spectacular show of power when it does. It usually hits home. Then, afterwards, they're able to chew on the situation after some quiet time. I love them up once again. I don't want to break their spirit or their confidence. As I get older, this becomes harder to pull off. I definitely feel it afterwards. It actually does hurt me more than it will ever hurt them!

In the business world where profit is the goal, many people get lost in this game. It becomes extreme. The rich and powerful usually partake in making the rules. It has been this way since the beginning of time. The world ends up with thugs ruling over their serfs, slaves, or servants of some kind. Always asking, "How do I earn more?"

Don't get me wrong; it's not all like this. There's some order in business today, with many good people and organizations out there all over the world. I can provide many names, but there are also many that succumb to the evil one … remember that serpent slithering about, reminding everyone about the profit motive. Profits are good, but not when they become a god and an end-all goal.

And if a particular person of power succumbs to the evil one, they become tyrants whether in the boardroom or out on the battlefield. Taking over with their ranting and raving. Basically whiny,

Chapter 4: Rekindling the Fire

selfish temper tantrums. Total opposite of what Jesus is trying to accomplish. Not coaching, always power grabbing with no loving up their people afterwards. Watch out. It will also affect the lowly and how they see and act in the world.

A good person of power will also affect their employees, soldiers, etc. Watch for the good here, for these people are living by example, too. This example will flow downstream, affecting how people below them see and act in this world as well. Until someone tries to take advantage of the goodness. The cynical refuse to see the goodness. Always geared up to take it down with their pessimism.

None of this is new. The Bible is full of examples of good and bad with their loss and redemption stories. What Our Father is attempting to do is instill trust and patience in each of us. Following Him with patience. Trusting in Him with patience. The world has never tolerated this at such a slow speed. It moves too fast. Evil moves faster, louder, and more obnoxiously. Sprinkling emotional overload all over us, suppressing our reason and logic. When in a fight between reason and emotion, sometimes we need a pep talk, at times extreme, pointing out our error. Toning down our emotional overload.

Seeing the corruption and people pushing God away, I'm inclined to go the route of Saint Benedict, too. Remembering my seventh-grade report on a saint. Saint Benedict is mine. He is the son of wealthy noble parents in about 500 AD. Young Benedict receives a great education at the time. The students in his class all have wealth and power but act out by choosing vice and worldly pleasures because they can. Benedict watches in disgust as these young students become adults and leaders in society, using their wealth for worldly pleasure on only themselves. He feels there is no choice but to withdraw from this world. It's only a devil's den rather than productive citizenry embracing God.

Benedict gives up his inheritance, moving outside of a small village in Italy, surrounded by peaceful solitude nature and our Father. Taking in the full gift of God's creation. Enjoying nature in the awe that it is. I find this very intriguing in the state I'm in right now. More than intriguing but darn right enticing. He builds the Monte Cassino Monastery in Italy from old ruins dedicated to Roman gods, becoming known for the Church's monastic system.

For me, not going to happen. I'm only thinking about me here because my intention is to walk away from it all. Then realizing my family needs me. Saint Benedict doesn't have little ones and a wife he loves depending on him already. With no mountain-man experience, I'd be dead in a week without God's help. This saint's intent is opposite of mine. He's hitting evil straight on. I'm only running away. God is depending on him to spread The Church. The truth must be advertised. It's necessary to save souls, bringing them all to God. Same as today.

Monasteries are outposts of civilization, helping the cause by spreading education, commerce, and God's Church throughout Europe, Asia, and Africa. Monks produce their own necessities with prayer and sweat equity. They are also the manual printing presses, reproducing scripture and translating manuscripts into numerous known languages. Again, a good thing. God never creates evil inside His Children or His Church. Repeating this is necessary for everyone to understand what we are all dealing with. It's not God's Church but man that produces sin.

Chapter 4: Rekindling the Fire

Any evil slithers its way inside individual men through holes in their armor of faith, deeply embedding itself unless something is done about it. Benedict sees this as a major caveat when saving souls. He is also known as "the protector against evil," standing right alongside Saint Michael and Our Lady in Heaven's battle against it. His medal features a shortened symbolic prayer used in the Rite of Exorcism. This small medal is inserted within the crucifix on my Rosary. Saying the name of Jesus with belief and meaning while holding the crucifix … I believe this saves me from being choked by evil's retaliatory efforts that early morning on December 21, 2020.

My point is that Saint Benedict says "Yes" when God asks him to follow. Giving up his wealth at a young age, he sees embracing the Father and "saving" souls as being the goal in all our lives. The world with evil, and how men succumb to it for whatever reason, will never save souls. Men have generations of Adam and Eve in their blood; they need Jesus to cast it out and drive it away. Living by example with the unshakeable faith of Saint Benedict saves souls for Heaven and Eternity. He shuns corruption of the time by picking up his cross and following Jesus.

One of the twelve apostles, Levi, also says "Yes" to Jesus when He asks the question. Levi is better known as Matthew. In Hebrew, it means "gift of Yahweh". I bring this up because Matthew is my Confirmation name. I had forgotten that I chose the name. Remembering when I find my Bible from Mom and Dad dated 1981. I recall three things; the red sash around my neck had white letters M-A-T-T-H-E-W glued to it. He is a tax collector, and I am worried the archbishop will yell at me in front of the whole congregation if he asks me a religious question I can't answer.

Dad is my sponsor, whom I have chosen. Ok, this is four things. Dad is a retired accountant, same profession as me. Dad and mom say "Yes" to Jesus when He calls them to follow Him as parents. Dad is a loving father in the light of Saint Joseph and a practicing Catholic, always leading by example. In addition to being a very smart businessman over the span of about forty-two years. I contend he does the right thing by people and his company. As I still run into people who know him. Always telling me a story about him with a genuine smile. Never giving me a look of slight.

Levi is a tax collector for the Roman Empire in the time of Jesus. Just like today, tax collectors are not always people we choose to hang out with. They have their place, and I'm sure many are good people. But there's always that thought in the back of most people's minds, "Did I just get cheated?" Especially after an audit. In Levi's person, this definitely is the case, the path he chooses for a while. It is an instilled mindset, saying three gold pieces for Rome, then one, maybe two gold pieces for me. Yes, he cheats and steals his way to wealth through his corruption, growing more abundant each year. He is a crony for the Roman government.

Then this life-style becomes a problem for Levi. When the Son of God, the Messiah, chooses him and asks, "Follow Me!" Jesus is smiling with His eyes staring at Levi, not blinking, waiting for an answer. Just like *Jesus of Nazareth*. He even knows who and what Levi is. He's categorized with the dregs of society, but he's also a "Blessed Child of God." That's where Jesus goes, looking for the downtrodden and lost souls in order to save the world with their help.

Jesus knows Levi better than he knows himself, his worries, his wants, his needs, and ultimately his regret for cheating people stirring around in his mind. "Follow Me!?" This question sure does the trick. Levi, I'm sure, is taken aback, thinking of all the wealth and prestige he's accumulated versus the accompanying guilt.

A fire builds inside Levi. The heat placing guilt and "I'm not worthy" to the forefront of his thoughts, eventually burning away these excuses. His fire will fully manifest itself on Pentecost, coinciding with all the other apostles, after Jesus Ascends into Heaven. At this point, he takes a leap of faith, giving it all up, saying, "Yes!" Becoming the Apostle Matthew.

He goes from a dishonest tax collector, counting coin and money, inhabiting the corruption in the "den of robbers" to a life of learning and teaching for the Master. He actually knows Jesus, personally, as a living man. Touching Him and listening to His words. Now, counting souls, saving people instead. Saving souls with the "Good News" he writes about in the first Gospel. His pride and indifference to corruption in society are both defeated by our Savior Jesus Christ.

This is the opposite of the "rich man" asking Jesus what he must do to inherit eternal life? The **Gospel of Mark 10:17-22** explains that Jesus tells him he must follow all of the commandments. The man exclaims that he has observed all of these. Then Jesus says to him, *"You lack one thing; go, sell what you have, and give it to the poor, and you will have treasure in Heaven; and come, follow me."* After Jesus finishes, the man goes away hanging his head, for he can't take this extra step.

Instead, Matthew is all in with following our Lord. For he gives up all of his stolen wealth, along with his pride. The "rich man" can't get over himself. The status he has achieved in this world is probably the biggest obstacle. Larger than all his money. He can't see himself hanging with the apostles. They look road traveled. Their feet are filthy. Their footwear appears used. Their clothes are dusty. He doesn't see the comradery and the happiness on all their faces.

I also count numbers, money for a living. An accountant by trade, my goal is when debits equal credits. Again, not a bad thing unto itself as commerce is accomplished with fair rules and regulations that everyone depends upon in the modern world. Providing order in God's Universe.

I love the numbers and explaining what they mean to others. That's the simplistic view. Unfortunately, it's not that easy. Even though I have about thirty-five years of business experience under my belt, it's working with people, co-workers, subordinates, bosses, Human Resources, and the executives making up the company where the real work is. This turns into a colossal mess at times when the goal is for the company to show a profit.

Most of the time you're dealing with too much ego and pride. Human Resources suggests substituting these negative attributes, putting together a company Utopia. Telling us we all have a best friend at work, and the entire company is one big happy family. This is lost when there's one little, itty, bitty hint of profits going south (profits bleeding red ink) or an executive that doesn't know how to communicate effectively and/or without the ability to lead.

Remember the whispering and shutting of doors? When this happens, everyone scurries in hundreds of different directions like ants. Then making their way back in a line, one by one, toward the middle of it all where they all commiserate together. It's instinct; they know no other way.

Chapter 4: Rekindling the Fire

This is nothing more than paranoia acting out. People are trying to convince as many people as possible that they are worthy of staying with the organization. Resulting in pleasantly, all legal of course, letting people go. The company turning into a Dystopia now. Nothing but a dysfunctional family with every employee for themselves.

I am one of those hypocrites. The path I chose! Is this corruption? When a company has many more options at their disposal to correct the problem of low profits. It's not always letting people go. Smart executives must earn their salary, presenting better alternative financial options. Letting people go is too easy. Especially when family is involved as defined by the company. Doesn't feel right to me. Sounds a little bit like collusion. You be the judge.

Truth is illustrated in Saint Benedict's choice giving up his wealth for Jesus. Embracing and pursuing our Father's Will even though he could have had a life of luxury. Also in Saint Matthew, who had lost truth by cheating and stealing. Only to regain it back again after Jesus comes into his life. Then there's my dad. As far as I can tell, this man has always had it. Personally, and in the business world. I see nothing to the contrary. All three are obedient when called!

We're all blessed … God creates Saints like Joseph, Benedict, and Matthew (and many more) as spiritual templates for all of us. Mom and dad are my own personal templates for me to follow. Their staunch faith in Jesus is fulfilled by their actions, keeping corruption and ultimately evil at bay. If these Heavenly templates are followed more often, Jesus doesn't have to yell out an emotional pep talk for all of us while overturning the tables of corruption in our temples.

Production

I am lost in translation when I produce without God. I miss the honesty of a hard day's work. The sweat, the exertion, my muscles aching in a good way. Evil rolls right off my back with good 'ole fashioned sweat.

Journal Entry January 2025

What are the money-changers producing in the temple when Jesus overturns their tables? Or is there no production going on, only the transfer of money for services? Jesus describes the scene as a "den of robbers" based on the fact His Father's House is being denigrated by people's commerce instead of creating reverence and prayer. The money-changers are selfish, stealing time from their Father, making money. Ultimately producing corruption and power, evil in the Temple of the Lord.

The ability to produce something viable for others is important on a national scale. One of the reasons the United States maintains its strength throughout its almost two hundred-fifty years of existence is the massive ability to produce. First agricultural products, then its abundant natural resources, manufacturing, producing buildings, structures, ships, etc., and individual religion with its good works for the country and individual souls.

It's a blessing endowed by our Creator, allowing all of this "rugged individualism" through our Constitution. During economic downturns or poor policy choices, the US still has the ability to produce in spite of itself, even helping countries less fortunate. Added bonus, the technology is there for farming and extracting natural resources in a clean fashion.

Most countries don't have this capability. They can't produce more than a few items, or they don't have the natural resources necessary to export to the world. Recessions and depressions almost destroy the people, taking many years to reestablish themselves again. Even worse for a country where its government clamps down on the means of production, individualism, and religion. When the state is in control of all these, this country eventually implodes upon itself. There's no production, and the debt increases to amounts with no hope of ever being repaid.

Individual people also produce ... or not. As an accountant, what do I produce? I sit behind a desk and count money, hearing a ding when debits equal credits—that's production for me. I even pat myself on the back—I'm so excited. When working for banks, I count time as interest accrues over months and years, sharing this accumulation with all the bankers. Or at a power plant, I count the energy produced then surging through the infrastructure to customers. I always take it seriously, taking pride in the results I present to the entire company.

Manual labor has been part of my portfolio of work, too. This includes cleaning offices, auto dealerships, warehouse work, and cutting lawns throughout my neighborhood. This is all busy work. These are my second, third, and forth jobs at times when I was younger. The production here is a completed service for your client or employer. The product is the manual labor, sweat equity, involved, adding to the virtue of providing for my family.

Saint Joseph and Jesus are carpenters. Lives of manual labor. Actually building something, producing it with their knowledge of the subject, their muscle, and sweat equity. I'm sure many of their creations are beautiful and well-received when finished. I'm also confident that evil is put off, running away when it sees people diligently performing hard work. Evil can't help but leave, rolling right off their bodies with their sweat equity, and the holiness in the case of Jesus and Saint Joseph.

Good works and prayer produce reverence to our Lord. Our goal as Catholics must be to trust Jesus and save souls with diligence. This is what gets lost in our busy lives of production, including mine. Pushing our Father away. Whether we produce too much or too little in our jobs, evil slithers its way back into our lives when we make it our golden calf. Or it can make us complacent, just going through the motions, as we appear busy to others just to get by.

Technology today is also doing this. We create business applications, building a type of new and improved company for all of us. Accounting is no different. CFOs want the latest and greatest software whether their company needs it or not. It's a prestige thing for them, making them a god in the company and the business world.

My worry becomes, do people know how to handle it when debits do not equal credits as supported by the app or software? Big question! Most of the time, the answer is no. Instead, you have groups just sitting around until IT fixes the problem. Or worse yet, the company is hacked and down for a week or two. Many accountants today wouldn't know how to sharpen a pencil and apply it to a journaled sheet of paper or use a ten-key calculator. Regardless of the new and

Chapter 4: Rekindling the Fire

improved software, we still need grunt accountants in line with good ole' Ebenezer Scrooge and his clerk Bob Cratchit.

Everything is continuously new and improved. Just update the app. Business and Accounting do it. Some feel Heaven is no different. In this case, Heaven is being defined by this world, no more suffering, no Jesus. Critical to Our Savior's message. I'm all for prayer apps for the beginner. At least these help people get started in the right direction. *Hallow* is a great prayer app tool! But if prayer and faith become fully based on an app, too, our brains then our faith turn into mush, as do our hearts. Our faith will grow dimmer and slowly be eliminated. Lost in the shuffle to simpler, easier, better. A prime target for evil.

We will still say the prayers, becoming only words, while in a comatose state, no meaning. It's not our hearts praying, talking to Jesus anymore. This becomes an app, too. Just like we still need grunt accountants, we need our reverence and faith staying in line with our human hearts. At a certain point, we will longingly say, "Oh how we will give up anything to get back to hard, manual labor from yesterday and producing a sound product with sweat equity, reverence to Jesus, and prayer."

Just wait until AI produces an answer from a request with … "God is an ambiguity not relevant in the current environment. A higher being cannot be proven. Miracles are only circumstance." Not much different than the verbiage of many intellectually endowed scholars when they don't take in the entire truth, right!

I've worked on many financial models. AI is only a model created by people. A large model pulling massive amounts of data from various sources producing an answer or a summary from a request.

Once programmed, the enter button is hit, producing the outcome. The outcome is a highly complex summary. Hopefully, the data created, as pulled, by all its sources is relevant. As in anything, the first question should be, "What is the goal of this exercise?" Please appreciate that humans have to program the code that defines the data and its sources.

Think of a model as an equation. Remember algebra—there is the x variable multiplied by a number, then possibly an additional y variable multiplied by a number, all producing answers. A model is only a multifaceted, outstretched algebraic equation. Finding answers to the given variables, or the final answer when the variables are given numbers.

No different with given weather models. Who hasn't experienced rain based on a sunny forecast the day before? As in everything, knowing the goal of the exercise from the outset is an ideal start. If man gets his hands on it, these can be manipulated, too. Model builders call it "tweaking" when they don't like the results. Algebraic facts turn into maybes. Models are only tools used to predict outcomes. God's children will never be able to predict the future with 100% accuracy!

My point is that "tweaking" can represent a number of either positive additions to the source data or possibly more of the model builders' biases. When AI models become the end-all answer in autonomy, our Catholic Faith must perform its due diligence and verify the sources of data involved. Remember evil produces nothing but evil, same with programming. Only God's Truth produces our salvation!

We are made to be dependent on God. He makes us in His image. He knows all of us individually better than we know ourselves. This dependence brings out the Mystery of Faith we are drawn to when embracing Jesus. We feel this Faith; it is ingrained in us. How do we measure this? Can we build in a special dependent variable that can measure this in our equation? Maybe by a permanent fixed number that always takes this into account? Something to be concerned about going forward.

Saint Thomas Aquinas is one of the most intelligent human minds I have come across in my religious studies. From what I find, he verifies our Faith with His passion for God, combining science, philosophy, and theology, proving the existence of God our Father. It is an outpouring of step by step easy to understand reason and logic. This is his concern in *"Summa Theologica"* written in the thirteenth century. A summary of our Catholic Faith up to that point. We add the emotion ourselves as we experience our Faith throughout our lives.

I think of Saint Thomas as the premier AI of the time, leaving behind artificial, replacing it with human intelligence. Using his mind with all of the data and its sources of the time allows all of us to follow his reasoning. This comes about based on books by *Kevin Vost* and *James F. Anderson*, summarizing Thomas' positions even more for us. This includes *Donald G. Boland, En Route* author. He has many books concerning these thoughts, summarizing the multifaceted into simpler faceted pieces, building them back up again. Producing Truth.

Same thing with video games. What is produced here? Entertainment, a little bit of happiness, if … IF, we take these for what they are. Games! Only a game to play when we have time. After our chores, work, and prayers are completed for the day. Instead, it is manipulated into a quasi-life, nothing to do with the reality we face each day. It gets really creepy when quasi-life scenarios are replicated into real-life. Look at all the quasi-humans after hours, or a days' worth of gaming, how do they look? Have they showered? How cluttered is their room? When brain mush is produced, evil takes over. Games can be conquered, real-life will always let people down unless they embrace Jesus.

Saying the *Hail Mary* and praying the *Our Father* as we do in the Rosary or at separate times produce devotion, held together by a relationship. We are reproducing holy times, by our thoughts and prayers which funnel down into our hearts and souls. Based on the lives of Our Mother and Her Son Jesus. All the glorious times, the joyous times, the luminous times, and ultimately the sorrowful times in their lives. When we think of them in our minds, quietly, or say them on our lips, loudly, they happen again. Start off slowly; it will expand tenfold in no time.

Producing these moments replay over and over again, each time Our Lady keeps Her foot snuggly placed on the head of the serpent. Celebrating the fact that these events are only but a moment ago, even though this has been going on for two thousand years. There must be something to this, not much lasts this long, if ever, in the memory of man. As he normally wets his finger, pointing it up, identifying which way the wind is blowing. Changing his stance as frequently as the wind blows.

Prayer consists of both heartfelt meaning behind the words and listening, attentively listening. When we pray, it's only considerate to

Chapter 4: Rekindling the Fire

allow our Holy Mother and Her Son to speak to us afterward. Heartfelt prayer should be on the same level of attentive listening. Listening is like winding down after exercise. So much more will be learned by everyone when we produce listening ... actual marching orders for the day or answers to our prayers. Attuned listening will allow understanding when others speak, too. A very efficient use of time when done properly.

Heaven fully opens up with the Baptism, the Passion, and the Resurrection of Jesus Christ. Christ's Ascension into Heaven shows us this, allowing God's children to enter. The love and mercy shown here is the definition of Heaven. Embracing Him by saying "YES" is the frosting on the cake, with full justice and judgment. Jesus knows we are sinners; evil is in the world. Our opportunity here is to be sorry, to repent, no matter how bad or how wicked we have been. In this sacrament, when we confess our sins to the priest, when we make reparations for our sins, we produce a clean soul. A new outlook taking advantage of what Jesus promises ... Heaven.

With our new outlook, we can participate in the sacrifice of the Mass. We produce the Last Supper again by attending as we should. We are in "communion" with Our Lord. This is more than a ceremony but a celebration for all of us. A party where a lamb is sacrificed and readied for a feast. Just like biblical times. With all of us present, the liturgy of the Word and the liturgy of the Eucharist combine into the new covenant we have with our Father. We break bread and drink wine. Jesus changes the bread into His Body and the wine into His Blood. We are filled with Him, Our Savior. Ready to take on the day or the week with Jesus inside of us.

The production of work, prayers, sacraments, graces and celebrations are for all of us, sinners and non-believers alike. Each time cuts into the evil one. Wounding it multiple times. Eventually, it will be obliterated, but right now we are at war. All because Our Lady says, "YES!" and evil with its legions say, "NO!" in the eyes of Heaven and Eternity. A very effective production cycle. If done right and followed through, worldly business managers can only envy! It is the Greatest Production Cycle ever put together.

Dangers of the World

With thousands upon thousands of different goals in this world, we are a mess. We have so many knots, tied up into a cob-web of evil. We are all knotted together just waiting for the world to untie us. That guy's sin will eventually affect me and visa-versa. Instead, we're waiting for evil to devour us. What if our goal turns into putting God first, getting to Heaven and Eternity? Yes, what if … ?

Journal Entry February 2024

Saving the souls of God's Blessed Children with the Truth is the goal of the Catholic Church. Welcome Jesus into your life. Pick up your cross. Follow Him. When lost, embrace His Mother. She will lead you back to Him. This is the plan to Heaven and Eternity no matter what the world conjures up. The path is all mapped out. Proven over the course of two thousand years. Sanctity can be achieved by all as long as the dangers of this world can be understood and then conquered.

> Beware of false prophets, who come to you in sheep's clothing but inwardly are ravenous wolves. You will know them by their fruits. Are grapes gathered from thorns, or figs from thistles? So, every sound tree bears good fruit, but the bad tree bears evil fruit. A sound tree cannot bear evil fruit, nor can a bad tree bear good fruit. Every tree that does not bear fruit is cut down and thrown into the fire. Thus, you will know them by their fruits.
>
> **Matthew 7:15-20**

Suffering Jesus Hanging on the Cross

There's a major piece of our Catholic Faith missing from the first paragraph? The suffering Jesus hanging on the cross. Our Lord crowned with thorns, bruised and bloodied with dry thirsty lips, looking at me with those same *Jesus of Nazareth* eyes, not blinking, waiting patiently for my answer when He asks, "Follow Me!?" Those piercing eyes looking through me now. He sees my guilt. My hesitation. My fear. Me. All I can do is cry!

Traveling with youth baseball teams finds me at various Catholic Churches on Sundays. Half of them have a genuine crucifix, like the one mentioned in the previous paragraph, hanging on the wall behind the altar. The other half portray toned-down smiling, happy Jesus with healed holes in His hands, His feet, and the slice in His side.

The disparity is interesting to a fault. Some even have both, which I don't mind, because all see both the sacrifice of Good Friday along with the Resurrection of Easter Sunday. It depends on the views of the pastor and the congregation. Defining how open they are to emphasizing the Truth in the Liturgy of Word and pouring out the actual sacrifice in the Liturgy of the Eucharist.

My parish portrays a very large suffering Jesus hanging behind the altar for all of us to see every time we celebrate the sacrifice of the Mass. I look forward to seeing this every Sunday. My focal point after the word is spoken and the Eucharist is consumed. The Truth is always right there in front of me. It's hard to miss unless not looking. All thanks to my pastor.

> Since therefore Christ suffered in the flesh, arm yourselves with the same thought, for whoever has suffered in the flesh has ceased from sin, so as to live for the rest of the time in the flesh no longer by human passions but by the will of God.
>
> **1 Peter 4:1-2**

The Passion of the Christ is a great reminder for us, focusing on the authenticity of what Jesus experienced during His Passion. Unfortunately, this film is over twenty years old now. Just like *Jesus of Nazareth* is almost fifty. It is already forgotten by the masses. The fact is we must have a continuous wheel of real reminders, keeping us excited about our faith. We need generation after generation of Christ's disciples, in their own unique way, reminding us all how this affects our in the moment current environment.

Chapter 4: Rekindling the Fire

The Chosen series does a great job showing both the apostles' real human relationship with Jesus blending in all their trials and tribulations. Based on the twelve, I can identify each of them by how they are presented. I have my own distinct picture of each one. And love going through the New Testament to see what is said about each. For what it's worth, reading the Bible is a good thing. Waiting on how they will handle the suffering of Jesus, which will be Season six. We are at Season five currently.

Jim Caviezel and *Jonathan Roumie* both play Jesus in these film adaptations. Both do a terrific job in their portrayal. Both are devout Catholics, taking the part seriously. Jim's movie is totally committed to the actual suffering Jesus experiences from the Agony in the Garden to the physical Resurrection in the tomb. Jonathan's series extends beyond Jesus, bringing in the humanness and the back-stories of all those close to him. Here we develop a relationship with all of them.

The toned-down Jesus is marketed to the world, worse is a pushed away Jesus, or worse yet, … NO Jesus. We have lost not only the crucified Jesus but the happy, smiling Jesus, too. No Jesus allows for politics, media, social media, Hollywood, this world to do whatever it wants without feeling guilty. The public sucks it all up. Man's truth isn't made in a day. No, it simmers in a pot over the course of years and decades.

After decades a new moral code develops. Virtue and discipline are no more. It is forgotten. Rules of etiquette become fascist or communist, depending on the politics involved. Who makes their beds anymore? How many days do dirty dishes sit in the sink? Let's "cancel" that rich guy because he hates that poor guy, who is a victim!

This morality doesn't need Jesus. Prideful man produces it and says, "Look what we did, we've evolved into our own religion! I can be "me" without Him!" And the world agrees.

Erasing the suffering Jesus hanging on the cross will not do. We need a constant reminder of what Our Savior does for us. The consequences of removing this are evident now. We're there. Without the suffering Jesus hanging on the cross, we don't have access to Heaven. The Heaven Jesus opened up when John baptizes Him. And the Heaven officially taking in God's children after we accept our own suffering with Him on Good Friday. It becomes like it never happened, if we push it away and forget it. It's not there without the suffering Jesus.

Mothers and Their Babies

One of my twin boys makes a statement to me I wasn't expecting. We're driving to school when the subject of abortion comes up on the radio. Both twins are in the car. He says in an excited statement in the form of a question, "What! … Abortion is killing a baby?" Obviously, he has no idea. He hears the term many times but doesn't understand what it actually is.

I automatically go back to before the twins are born. My wife and I do have some skin in the game here. Madeline is born at twenty weeks. Forty weeks is a full term baby. We take it seriously when the doctor diagnoses a problem. She is not what they call a "viable" pregnancy. Meaning she will not survive outside the womb. Madeline is going to be born early no matter how hard the doctors try to keep her in the womb. With water already broken and her entering the birth canal, Madeline is born in her mother's arms while I'm running around trying to find a nurse or a doctor on August 11, 2010. She has everything to remain viable except her lungs.

I've heard many stories about these type of births. This is me digging deeper into the truth so that I get it correct. I've been burned too many times before. Some Face Value narratives will call this an abortion, too, lumping it into a positive statistic for their cause. Becoming health care, a mass of cells, a zygote, and maybe a fetus. Put a check in all four categories. All to prove a point. Totally ridiculous and illogical. And sick as far as I'm concerned.

Madeline's mother doesn't have a choice in this case. Her only choice is to birth a viable Madeline. God's Will is to have Madeline in Heaven with Him. It's hard, but we trust and accept His choice. Remember, He will make up for it a year to the day later when He gives us two babies. I turn to my twin, look at him a bit puzzled and reply, "Yes, it's killing a baby." … This one's all on me! We discuss the subject further.

> Truly you have formed my inmost being; you knit me in my mother's womb. I give you thanks that I am fearfully, wonderfully made; wonderful are your works. My soul also you knew full well; nor was my frame unknown to you when I was made in secret, when I was fashioned in the depths of the earth. Your eyes have seen my actions; in your book they are all written; my days were limited before one of them existed.
>
> **Psalms 139:13-16**

I have never really discussed the subject fully with anyone except my wife. To me, abortion has always been wrong. I have always had a tender spot for all the babies that have endured this suffering. Every morning, I ask Our Lady to keep them all close to Her heart, praying for them to obtain Heaven soon.

Likewise, there is a tender spot of mercy for all mothers of aborted babies. I pray for their well-being every morning, too. Treating the mother with any type of indifference is wrong. To lovingly convince her otherwise should be attempted. It's not just one or the other, the mother or the baby, it's both of them going through this extreme event together. They are mother and child. They are one. Mother Mary and Jesus prove this by both of them suffering for our sins. How can there be a division or a separation?

The aborted baby is always a victim of decisions beyond its control. No if's, and's, or but's about it. This aborted baby has no choice! It is subject to the decision of their mother. There's no argument to this fact. Again, some people might call the baby, health care, or a clotted mass, or give it a more honorable name of zygote, maybe fetus. Regardless of word play, this miracle not there before conception, is abruptly terminated.

> If you want to avoid judgment, stop passing judgment. Your verdict on others will be the verdict passed on you. The measure with which you measure will be used to measure you.
>
> **Matthew 7:1-2**

I'm not going to argue against the mother having a choice. What I will say is, "I'm a sinner, too." There are so many loathed circumstances beyond the mother's control and/or excuses out there that a mother can use. Some happen more often than others and some are so terrible most of us can never imagine. The fact is abortion is legal in the United States and will not change unless there is at minimum sixty members of either party in the US Senate. These are voted in members to this chamber of Congress. No matter how much I abhor it and pray for an end to it, this is sadly the case. The situation this country is in.

> But Jesus, aware of their malice, said, "Why put me to the test, you hypocrites? Show me the money for the tax." And they brought him a coin. And Jesus said to them, "Whose likeness and inscription is this?" They said, "Caesar's." Then he said to them, "Render therefore to Caesar the things that are Caesar's, and to God the things that are God's."
>
> **Matthew 22:18-21**

The mother has a choice. There's no argument here either. Unless there is truly a health issue as in the case of Madeline. But I will always gently suggest another option to abortion no matter the circumstances the mother is facing. **The Ignatius Catholic Study Bible** goes further. In summary, Jesus is telling us we are created in God's image. Further implying, we should fulfill civic duties under the law, but it is our duty of giving ourselves back to God and His rules, serving God must be our primary obligation.

This is such a touchy subject that can turn nuclear at any time. So much emotion rather than cooled heads abound. This is why I've embedded all of these Bible verses. I need to reinforce our Catholic belief. First of all, only our judicial precedence, not our laws, have given the go ahead for abortion. But the judicial branch can't pass laws! That's only a designated duty of Congress per the US Constitution. Secondly, shame on those misaligning this important aspect of our country.

Here's an interesting hypothetical that did actually happen … with the creation of AI and new technology, what if, what IF, … the baby is given the choice of choosing its own mother? That's exactly what happens when God makes His choice. His Mother says, "YES!" Accepting all of the worldly and Heavenly consequences. No AI necessary.

The correct answer comes down to asking – What is your goal in life? … How will this decision affect (1) your body and your baby's, and (2) your life and your baby's? Ultimately, how will this decision affect your Heaven and Eternity? Which time period is longer? Do you really deep down trust this world? Bottom line – our goal must change; God's Law always surpasses our worldly law!

> Before I formed you in the womb I knew you, before you were born I dedicated you, a prophet to the nations I appointed you.
>
> **Jeremiah 1:5**

It is written, all of God's children are viable under Heaven. Whether they have the privilege of being born into this world or not. Here the choice is God's only. Nothing in this world can override Our Father's Plan – evil, sin, selfishness, nothing. The final chapter will explain from my perspective the "power" God's children have while living in this world if they only embrace Him. God has the "final choice" in the reality of His creation, along with His Heaven and Eternity.

Creating Our Own gods

God sprinkles little pieces of Heaven upon His creation as gifts, helping us sustain our faith. Absorb the beauty of our world, the sky, mountains, and the colors within a beautiful sunset. Or perhaps our families, the opportunities our country provides, celebrate the victories like Alveda King suggests. Our own talents – once found these can be life-changing, sharing them with others is the Heaven. Our Father is not one of these gifts, He is in all of them because He creates them for us!

> I, the Lord, am your God, who brought you out of the land of Egypt, that place of slavery. You shall not have other gods besides me. You shall not carve idols for yourselves in the shape of anything in the sky above or the earth below or in the waters beneath the earth; you shall not bow down before them or worship them.
>
> **Exodus 20:2-5**

With the evil one slithering about, we have a tendency to go further than God's intent. When we push Him away, we take these gifts and selfishly turn them into something beyond their purpose. Stealing them away into something we own. Easy enough when they're given to us freely out of love and mercy. No effort on our part but to enjoy.

Most people have goals or more importantly lifelong dreams they are working toward. The thought usually takes hold of a person at a young age based on experience or their upbringing. How grounded they are in reality and truth, or not, are also big pieces. Everyone is different, unique, by family-line, by gender, be geography, by talents, etc. Some have enough fire in the belly to pursue, never giving up. Others, not so much. Dropping their quest after they get hit in the mouth a couple times. In many cases this becomes the pursuit of filling some type of void or want in their lives that the world embellishes.

Goals and dreams become extreme when they become the only thing driving a life. Here we fail to realize our Father makes us all up with many intricate pieces. We place our God-made self aside, failing to investigate all of our pieces, replacing them all with our man-made self. When this doesn't play out the way we want it to, we are sad, turning into anger at Jesus. We place this goal or dream above God; it is now our god. I am no different.

Think about how you spend your time. We are time-constrained by twenty-four hour days. That's all we have per God. Does your time have to do with a dream? A goal? A game? These are alright as long as the family is taken care of, chores are completed, and worship is performed. Or is it something within yourself? Work? Having a good time? Sex? What are you pursuing that pushes God away, hiding Him? The items and their damaging consequences are endless.

Evil can turn anything good into something bad. It places alternate perceptions into people's heads that have nothing to do with God's intent. Pouncing on the emotion involved. As proven by the words I write in my journals.

Take youth sports. Over the last twenty-five years, I've either coached or parented my boys and girls in baseball, basketball, soccer, volleyball, and dance. The last decade turns our youth playing amateur "fun" games into aggressive winner take all competitions. More time, more money, more travel, and yes, more disappointment. Not to mention the additional doctor bills. Parents incentivize this behavior. In many cases they are playing through their kids, saying, "I couldn't go pro, but my kid will!" Another god being worshiped.

It's great; kids with these activities tend to stay out of trouble and learn how to handle winning and losing … or life. My boys have great coaches, mentors and men. But families are giving up other pieces of themselves and their environment. Learning suffers. Family time is constant fast food with all of the wrappers thrown away. How many doubleheaders are scheduled on Sunday? When is there time for God and what He requests from us? He gets scheduled less and less, drifting into a distant memory. In this instance, a fun game becomes a god now.

Today, we are so into ourselves, making it difficult to see anything or anyone else. It becomes the norm, not realizing our errors until it's too late. Right Covid-19! Once we've attained our prestige, our job, our money, our own children in good schools, etc., we want to keep it all. Even at our own detriment to salvation. We forget everyone is a Blessed Child of God. This is the "dark side" of America's rugged individualism. Our blessings are not shared, becoming an over-reaching god at times.

Don't get me wrong. I'm all for rugged individualism. With this privilege we are not exceptional, or better than everyone else, but we are the exception, allowing us to be our true selves backed by a Constitution of freedom. The first country of its kind. With reverence toward God, we can be anything we want within His plan for us.

Without our Father we go off into tangents of ourselves, taking advantage of world aspirations. Humility doesn't grow in this environment. It becomes weaker as evil takes over, growing it into pride, ego, control, and/or selfishness.

Take being a parent. A blessing under God. We are parenting not only our children but God's children. A job that should never be taken lightly. Because now we're talking about another person's Heaven and Eternity, too. This is living by example, not trying to make my kid better than your kid that is scene today. Exemplified by moving my three younger boys to new schools during Covid. A lot of in-your-face parents refusing to live up to our Parent-pact.

The beauty of a woman can capture a man's heart as he professes his love to her. Emotion turns into the silliness of a child, a sort of giddiness when she turns around and feels the same. It can stop here or develop into both of them caring for each other's well-being under Heaven – here, emotion and reason combine, becoming God's gift as a married couple. The man and the woman then make each other the best they can be with a goal of Heaven and Eternity.

When I look at my wife, this is what I see. Something I've prayed for since watching Elvis movies at the age of seven. I've never lost that silliness of a child as she can attest to. My prayers are answered with Constance. This is my piece of Heaven on earth with the added bonus of seven children and grandchildren.

I tell my boys women are special, every one of them. Always remember they all have fathers that love them and want the best for them. Being a good man and finding a good woman is important for all of us as God's children. Going further, "Do not use them or abuse them!"

Pornography is just that. Evil at its (un)finest. Every man will have unholy thoughts in their minds throughout their lives. How you handle these thoughts is important to your Eternity. And beware of the women that will lead you down this evil path, too. When emotion stops at lust, men can go down some pretty dark paths, becoming an unholy god. I've been there a time or two.

It comes down to humility and the pride one carries around with them. And the confidence we have in our Blessed Mother. Embrace Her. Start off slowly. People can worship thousands of different gods without even knowing it. Easy to do with all the "noise" we hear in this world. Slow down and listen. Well-being is a thing. Can it be kept? Keeping it is a daily fight? Sometimes, even a minute-by-minute fight with evil. The "weapon" of choice is the Rosary!

Face Value Idealism

Looking into a mirror, you are standing in front of everything behind you. In this instance, all you can see is yourself. A face and an upper body, maybe the entire self, reflecting back at you. The story of standing in front of a mirror is … You. That's all you see. Using this context, any story you write about will be about you. Literally Face Value Idealism.

Face Value Idealism and its narrative was initially discussed in Chapter one. Journaling opens my eyes to this form of control and misapplication of the truth. This applies to our faith, our reverence to Jesus more than anything else in today's environment. Again, it's easy to apply. Going down the definition of quasi, previously established as mocked up, you can appear intellectual while using everyone's emotion. Blowing it up, emphasizing the intended scheme. Ultimately, becoming a quasi-intellectual is mocking our God-given reason and logic.

Using this form of "untruth" as a means to an end is allowed to happen because we live in the United States. We hear this in most of the politics and its activism, in some of the journalism and media, in a selection of authors and their books, and in most social media. Here's a little secret to chew on and digest, true communists, fascists, and all tyrants, drum roll ... *do not allow this, it's forbidden, these forms of government will put you in jail and/or kill you!* The U.S. Constitution enables its citizens free speech. All under God! As bad as this can get, it's up to God's children to decipher, if they want all the good and bad outlined for them when defining the truth.

Dive into the subject, dive in as far as you can go. Don't rely on political hacks or media weasels to provide the information. Don't take their certification when they fact check anything. Most of them will only tingle your senses above the surface. Become an expert on the subject yourself. There are a lot of resources available to everyone in our tech-based world. Read diaries, journals, and writings from important people in history. See where they actually stand. Truth

Chapter 4: Rekindling the Fire

deserves this. Better yet, God deserves this. His people are thirsting for it.

I believe this is the most perilous of our dangers in this world. Just about everything, including the items aforementioned in this section, can be manipulated to one's cause with propaganda and quasi-truth using this narrative. We are marketing heaven on earth.

> Give heed! For noble things I speak; honesty opens my lips. Yes, the truth my mouth recounts, but wickedness my lips abhor. Sincere are all the words of my mouth, no one of them is wily or crooked; all of them are plain to the man of intelligence, and right to those who attain knowledge. Receive my instruction in preference to silver, and knowledge rather than choice gold.
>
> **Proverbs 8:6-10**

Take the term social justice as just one example. Pope Leo XIII (the 13th) expresses concern for the poor and the less fortunate as they're being lost in transition to the Industrial Age. Coining the phrase "Social Justice" in 1891. His intent is to make government aware of their suffering. Just as Upton Sinclair and his book *The Jungle* accomplishes. In addition to prodding the Catholic Church to do more in their plight, giving them all hope for a better life. Asking, "What would Jesus do!?"

Pure and simple "Social Justice" starts with being transparent. The poor are miserable, whether they are sharecroppers in the south, picking weeds in between rows of corn, or working in a meat packing plant. The Catholic Church is requested to help the workers cause. Not only saving souls, but saving souls *and* giving them hope for a good life while raising their families.

Just mention the plight of the poor brings out emotions in people. No one wants to see their fellow man miserable. Local governments get more involved, passing laws helping the workers plight. Better working conditions and better pay. Eventually, the federal government does, too. Not perfect, but then again America isn't. We have to trust in the Father's Will.

Mid-Twentieth Century, "Social Justice" becomes politics. Evil and its minions take advantage of people's emotions. It gets complicated and evil is in the details, becoming a system where well-rooted politicians and activists funnel money into their own pockets. Again, the accountant in me says follow the money and you will find the corruption where disingenuous people are taking advantage of the poor. Who would ever think that people can get rich just by saying they're with the "social justice" division? They'll even shove their "social justice" ribbon or pin on their suit lapel in people's faces, saying, "See, see, look at me, I'm so good!"

Sorry to be so truthful … uh, no I'm not because it makes me sick. But I will apologize to the "true" social warriors, the brothers and sisters of charity. The selfish use God and His people's emotion. Legalizing theft, like my child support. One area we need to get back to is the definition of pure "Social Justice" that Pope Leo XIII requests from us. Here the goal is actually helping the poor and downtrodden, lifting them up. Pray the Rosary for … TRUE, "Social Justice!"

We are all temples on earth, rich or poor. Holy Spirit please burn down the corruption cycle of "social justice" people have developed and expand charity, empathy, and the truth. Like Jesus did two-thousand years ago in the temple. Tear the evil down, get politics out of it. Build it back up, working along with the true, genuine "Social Justice" warriors of today that don't need a pin or a ribbon on their chest. Being anonymous like Saint Nicholas is warranted, too. Politics get out, selfish people of prestige aren't fit for the job!

One of the belongings of my Grandma Bluvas is her book *The Catholic Family Book of Novenas* dated 1956 published by John J. Crawley & Co., Inc. In order to help us identify Face Value Idealism and its narrative today, we must take into account the gifts of the Holy Spirit. Here we refresh our God given logic and reason, bringing this gift back up in-line with our emotion. Just like we clear our cache in our computers, we have to eliminate too much built-up emotional overload. Making our person more in line with our Father's intention.

Reading "The Seven Gifts of the Holy Spirit" takes out the dangers of this world, isolating them into what they are ... evil's obstacles to Heaven and Eternity. Every morning, I pray for mastery of all these gifts. All of these are relative to our world today, just as they were back in 1956. Rekindle my fire of truth burning within me. Keep it burning, Michael!

These seven gifts of the Holy Spirit are ideal to rationalize the dangers of this world. I pray that I utilize all of these gifts every morning. Thank you, Grandma Bluvas!

Prayer for the Seven Gifts of the Holy Spirit:

Wisdom ... that I may despise the perishable things in this world and aspire only after the things that are eternal.

Understanding ... to enlighten my mind with the light of Thy divine truth.

Counsel ... that I may ever choose the surest way of pleasing God and gaining heaven.

Fortitude ... that I may bear my cross with Thee and that I may overcome with courage all the obstacles that oppose my salvation.

Knowledge ... that I may know God and know myself and grow perfect in the science of the Saints.

Piety ... that I may find the service of God sweet and amiable.

Fear ... that I may be filled with a loving reverence towards God and may dread in any way to displease Him.

The Catholic Family Book of Novenas, page 97, 1956

Dangers in this world are man created with the help of the serpent. Again, our Father will never create destruction or anything without love and mercy. All of His creations are good, reflecting Heaven. Our Catholic Church and the United States were never created to support anything evil. It is men within each of these creations succumbing to sin. He will weed out the darkness on His time. Just as He has over the last five-thousand years in the Bible.

I think of myself when my oldest, Zachary, is born. One of the reasons I look into the military. Finances, school, and housing are a big decision factor at the time. At twenty-one, I succumb to the evil one and panic. This didn't and shouldn't see the entire Bluvas-family name as corrupted. No, this is the proven corruption of only one person, Michael Bluvas, within the Bluvas family. Here, I reach out to Jesus and Saint Joseph, too. Going to school and working many jobs, supporting my children. Sacrificing under God with love changes even the most hardened heart.

Evil sometimes takes over priests, popes. Unfortunately, people's perception becomes warped when this happens. They see it as Catholicism is corrupt not only the Church. Not just some of the people within it. Same as the United States. Our nation is not corrupt, but yes there are corrupt leaders, politicians, activists, and news media that form the perceptions of some people. All because evil pounces on men and women within. Or since we are all susceptible to sin, maybe it's a good priest or good politician on a bad day?

Chapter 5

FIRE POWER

When the day of Pentecost had come, they were all together in one place. And suddenly a sound came from heaven like the rush of a mighty wind, and it filled all the house where they were sitting. And there appeared to them tongues as of fire, distributed and resting on each of them. And they were all filled with the Holy Spirit and began to speak in other tongues, as the Spirit gave them utterance.

Act 2:1-4

Reconciled

Accountants take notice of the word "reconcile". This means taking two pieces, segments or accounts, calculating what goes into each of them, numbers right! What item separates them from being equal? In God's case, what goes into man and earth, comparing them to Heaven? This will tell us, as we prove it out, the difference is Jesus. This will make earth equal to Heaven. Jesus is the reconciling item.

Journal Entry March 2025

An Income Statement identifies funds coming into a company, calling them revenues, and funds going out, calling them expenses.

At year-end, more revenue leads the company to a profit. Hopefully, there's more recognized revenue than incurred expenses. Usually budgeted for with this in mind. This statement is pretty straightforward when following the rules and regulations of GAAP.

Then there's the company Balance Sheet. This statement is more mysterious. Non-accountants would say shadowy. What makes up the company. All of its assets, what it owns, all of its liabilities, what it owes, and all profits or losses kept over the years of operation. This is where accountants and their companies can get into trouble without rules and regulations. Thank you, GAAP! But anyways … all accounts within this statement must be reconciled to verify their validity. Because bad stuff can still be going on even if debits equal credits.

Now, bear with me … all profits on the Income Statement at the end of the year are closed because the year is complete. Then written over to the Balance Sheet. Additions are good, helping the company grow every year. But, losses reduce the company. Too many year-over-year losses cause the company to implode. It can't be sustained. If this is the case, then no more company.

This is where our faith is as individuals. Our Income Statements are crippled by mounting expenses (worldly goals, pride, wealth, etc.) coupled with realizing less and less revenue (God's graces, humility, patience, virtue, etc.). Every year, our losses are more than our profits. We budget every year in this world, playing God, for individual profits, failing to realize we are under God's GAAP.

Instead, one by one, group by group, country by country, we are imploding. God's children are imploding, blowing up all by ourselves. Because of the evil one pouncing on us. We sell off any remaining assets for pennies on the dollar; evil buys them up. Owning our souls now.

Jesus Christ our Savior is that "reconciling item" necessary. God invests His Son in our world. All for us to remain a "going concern" or a stable ongoing person with a soul. Reuniting us back to God and Heaven. He is our missing link in this world. Keeping us all profitable forever in God's GAAP. His environment working in all its order, fairness, and judgment. The only place true love and mercy meet head on with true equity and justice, making everything fair for all of God's children.

Jesus gives us the Sacrament of Reconciliation or Penance. Here we as Catholics, when we lose our reconciling item, Jesus, because of sin, can confess these sins to a priest or Jesus' delegate. We hit the "do over" button, making devote reparations for our sins. And we can move on with a clear conscience, sharing again the graces bestowed upon us.

I remember each one of my children's First Confessions. I was right there in line with them. Afterwards, they are all "giddy" with happiness. It's truly amazing to see. Caitie and Caela are both stoked with the Holy Spirit, laughing uncontrollably. Something they still do to this day. Running around in circles and laughing while hugging my leg. It is so cute as the giddiness infects me, too. The twins are messing around with a couple friends in their confessional line. I grab each of them by the neck (not too tight but enough to show I mean business) and place them ahead of me. Nothing but Holy with folded hands afterwards. Their friends do the same behind us, too.

After we confess, we are in "Communion" with Jesus. Able to share in the sacrifice of the Eucharist. Here, since we actually receive

Jesus, as He is the sacrifice, we have to be without mortal sin. Otherwise, it blows up in our face. Meaning we don't receive the graces or Him. We are misaligned. He is pure love and mercy. In a state of sin, we can never mix with the attributes of Heaven. Pure love and mercy cannot absorb anything sinful.

Hence, the Sacrament of Reconciliation is literally the reconciling item, allowing us to be combined with Jesus here on earth. As a man, that's what God does for His children. The result of His Passion and His Resurrection.

Every morning as part of my prayers, I pray for the people I've hurt and sinned against throughout my entire life. I am heartily sorry. I pray that they can find it in their hearts to forgive me and give it to Jesus. I pray they can place this hurt and sadness that I have created under Jesus' cross, giving it to Him. I pray for them to absorb His light and find His Spirit, then make reparations for their own sins, finding their own path to Heaven and Eternity.

Unfortunately, this is all I can do. I can't go back and fix it. But I can confess it all in the Sacrament and go forward, living by example, not doing it again. Oh, how I try not to! I don't like a sad Mother Mary, or Her Son. I don't want to push the thorns around their hearts even more. But with this world and evil, it's always easier said than done. My goal is to go to Confession every month or at least every couple months.

Going through the Confession line can also be part of the reparation process. The priests are busy. There are scheduled times where it is offered throughout the week. Know these times, memorize them, and be ready when necessary.

When I go during the week, lunchtime, there usually is a pretty good line. I am under a time constraint with my schedule, too. This feels like a long, slow, agonizing, ... purgatory. Waiting in line, hoping I can get into the confessional before Father has to stop and leave for Mass. Just like the agony when in a line of traffic, attempting to merge into a clear lane.

Ok. Sit there without fidgeting. Pray. Don't complain. Accept it. Offer all of your anguish and your torment going on inside your head to Jesus as a reparation. I try ... but not always successful. Then I think about what I'm in line to do.

The double-masked lady in the grocery store is owed an apology. I didn't handle the situation like I should have. It was too abrupt because I felt trapped on top of my financial situation. She nudged me, whether it was truth or not. If anything, we could have had a conversation. I didn't take into account her feelings and what she was experiencing at the time. I only thought about myself. Bottom-line, I'm sorry for this situation.

I am also sorry for the ill-will I conjured up in my thoughts when dealing with all of the customer service people I ran into with our debt and when our vehicle was repo'ed. The repo guy and his company, the vehicle customer service person, and the wire-guy. The sheriff. And even parents that can't seem to abide by our parent-pact when raising children. A true confession was made with all of this in mind.

Once complete, my cache is cleared from my operating system. My soul is more efficient and able to handle the world on God's terms. I am more apt to perform acts of humility and charity. Definitely more patience and control, focusing more on Jesus. There's the giddiness and sense of well-being. I'm a child again. Yes, every time. A miracle? ... Oh yeah!

One of the sins most confessed, glaring us all right in the face, has to be talking gossip about our neighbor. This happens all the time without that neighbor being present. It can be therapeutic to share little issues with others when stating facts. Most of the time these are blown-up issues from only our perspective ... where is the neighbor's point of view, their perspective? There lies the problem, talking behind another person's back.

It's easy to do, getting caught up in a good ole' fashion bitch session. I've gotten taken away in these, and I've even started them. Yes, I admit, I've been a gas-lighter. These blow up into telling lies about people, as the stories grow bigger and bigger with emotion for emphasis. If the stories are told with emotion, they've got to be true. Doing this, eventually I find my stomach growling, making me sick. Telling me no ... Stop!

The best way to handle these instances is to tell others, "I have no comment, as I'm not one-hundred percent sure of the facts here." Or something to this point. Then finding something else to do, picking up and walking away. It's not good to just sit there in silence and let it happen, appeasing it, either.

Usually, these instances are products of people – neighbors, God's children, that you see as impeding you from getting something you want. Your pride takes over. In war both sides degrade their foe, demonizing them, making them anything else but human. This is no different. Relating every bad habit or body shaming any of their ugliness whether true or not. Telling ourselves, "See that guy or gal is an idiot!" Because he's too fat or too skinny, too dumb or too smart.

Something you're not. Ask yourself are you may be a bit jealous? C'mon be truthful here!

I have degraded my neighbor's good name. Getting over my prideful self is hard. The world eats this stuff up, saying it's ok to talk positive about yourself then turn around and talk smack about another's reputation. Poor lost soul I am, we all are. Remember your reason and logic must be in line with your emotion in order to find the truth. Let's find humility and the truth when we're all together so everyone can speak.

Come to Jesus Moments

Patrick comes home for a visit from Marine boot camp in March of 1988, fit and confident. You could tell his demeanor has changed. He is more direct with his comments. Ready for anything. I am proud of my little brother. And ready for my own transformation in the Army! Little did I know my transformation wouldn't occur for almost 40-years.

Journal Entry April 2025

Going to Jesus can be done at any time. Every day, I set my cell alarm for 3 pm. The hour He passed on Good Friday. I want to set time for Him in my busy day. The alarm helps because otherwise I will forget. I use the time to do exactly what this section suggests. The actual meaning behind the title highlights the fact that at various times throughout my life I need to learn a lesson about either something bad I continue to do and/or something under my consciousness I'm not aware of. These moments are not necessarily good as they are some kind of awakening to reality.

Come to Jesus Moment, number 1 – My stint in the Army is only about six-weeks. It is a total flop! I go from flying high with pride and confidence, knowing how to fix my problems at a young age, to a deflated piece of humility.

I am six foot, and fat at twenty-one only a few years after highschool. Once I arrive, the pounds fly off. The first five days go well because we aren't allowed to talk on the phone. Meaning not much drama to take in from back home. Starting the second week, I am held back because of my weight. I have to lose more weight with a week of physical training only. Disappointing, but I hang in there. This gives me time before lights out to make a five-minute phone call each night. Somehow, I know this is a bad idea …

All I'm going to say is after about a week of phone calls my mind is so stuffed full of drama and whine-infested theatre, … it explodes. This is the point in my goal where I get punched in the mouth a couple times and essentially withdraw from training. The quest is done fore. I am not a warrior, no more fire in the belly. Partly my fault with the extra pounds and partly the phone calls home. Regardless, my time in the Army is short, and I'm a civilian again. I become subjugated to my world of drama, selfishness, and no-control. I do this all to myself, my choice. Realizing my mom was right!

Come to Jesus Moment, number 2 – My twins and I are eating lunch at a local fast-food restaurant, finishing up. When we hear a disturbance in the back of the small restaurant. At first, it sounds like a guy throwing up his liquid lunch. It becomes louder as he makes his way to the front in full view of all the patrons. I try to defer the

Chapter 5: Fire Power

boys' attention on me, but I can see their young eyes bulging with questions as they keep shifting toward the noise.

Once the guy reaches the front, I see his hands clutching his throat, trying to get someone to help him. I finally figure out, "He's choking!" Another guy takes charge running toward him. This guy is a lot smaller but grabs him around the back anyways, squeezing him a couple times right below his sternum.

My reaction is to just let it be. My own eyes look down, gazing on our own table. In the hope that the disturbance will fix itself and just go away. Nope… after a couple squeezes the smaller guy realizes he can't help the bigger guy stop choking. The smaller guy is older, sees me out of the corner of his eye, saying, "Get up and help this guy … c'mon move it!" Almost yelling at me to get off my butt.

This kick in the butt gets me out of my chair. I hurriedly pass by the other tables. I easily place my arms behind the poor guy. And I squeeze right under his sternum. Next time, squeezing and picking him up off his feet. Again, and again. I pretend it's Patrick and we're playing around in the house. I am actually pissed based on my non-action. Not sure how many times I pick him up and squeeze, but it works. The guy lays there on the ground sitting up against the front counter with his teeth plate in has hand that is almost sucked down his throat when eating his hamburger.

He looks up and says, in a hard to translate raspy voice, crying, "Thanks, so much!" I give him a hug, tearing up myself. I can tell by his expression he is so thankful someone helps him. I'm no hero; I was going to let him die! The ambulance arrives, taking over from there.

I look around for the older gentleman that kicked me in the butt to help. As I wanted to thank him. Expecting him to scorch me again. He is nowhere to be found. Not in the back, not in the bathroom, not in the kitchen, nor outside in his car. Nowhere. Devine intervention? Don't know. I need to carry this with me though.

"C'mon boys, let's go!" They are still trying to figure out what just happened, as am I. Their eyes still bulging. The only thing I say to them when we get to the car is, "I should have moved faster to help that man. I'm glad he's ok!" They agree. I say nothing more. Hopefully, they learn something about helping others when called upon.

This event is another failure, but it starts a little fire in me. A come to Jesus Moment I have been waiting my entire life for up to that time. In other words, pick yourself up, get off your butt, and follow Jesus. Not just on Tuesdays and for part of the weekend but always. Don't just follow your dreams or your wants.

These two events in my life are two smaller "Come to Jesus Moments" teaching me a little about failure. Believe me there are more as I've previously mentioned, but these are more profound for me. Failure definitely doesn't feel good when in the moment. The intent is for failure to hang with you, stick with you, then learn from it. Disappointing and alarming for the sheer fact others have seen me fail. Then, ultimately, allowing me to grow from it for next time. Again, divine intervention … it's got to be!

Mother Mary leads me back to Her Son, Jesus on Easter Sunday, 2021. Her promise is fulfilled. Jesus tells me to Trust in Him … and forgive. The "forgiveness" is that something missing inside me from His message. I ask for forgiveness when I hurt or sin against someone else, taking advantage of Confession. I'm also drawn to the *"Our*

Father" asking us to, "Forgive those that trespass against us!" Just like Pope John Paul II did when he forgave his shooter. Again, there's power in being able to forgive!

Our Church Pastor is a wonderful priest. Inviting all of us to partake in the Catholic education he brings to the Parish. One Sunday he brings in a priest he knows for the sermon after the gospel that is well-experienced in spiritual warfare against evil. Telling a story about miracles and how they relate to actual forgiveness. Father has my full attention. He tells the story about a nun he knows suffering from years of debilitating back pain.

Father meets her on an evangelical mission to Africa. The first time he encounters Sister, Father sees her suffering. But after speaking with her for a while, he realizes she is harboring ill feelings toward her own father that only invites evil into her life. It has been fermenting in her for years because of his lifestyle brought on from drinking. He is still alive, so she calls him. They meet the next day, producing an outpouring of forgiveness and tears, washing the evil away. They end in a good place with an added bonus of Sister walking without pain the next morning.

I have quite a few instances within these five chapters where I need to forgive those people who have hurt me and sinned against me. "Come to Jesus Moments!" The only way to do it properly is to tell the truth. Not using Face Value Idealism as the fireworks below need to do their thing in bringing them all together.

Come to Jesus Moment, number 3 – Learning how to forgive is the most difficult thing I must do. After hearing Father's sermon about "forgiveness" and how it can cripple our own Faith, I ask,

"How is this affecting me?" I think about the people and organizations that have hurt me.

Truthfully, this is only me feeling the above the surface half-truths of Face Value Idealism that I've previously warned others about. I'm only looking into a mirror at myself. To fully divest myself from this hurt and act on forgiveness, I've got to see the fireworks going off below the surface. Take the emotion out of it, pairing it with my reason and logic, and God's mercy.

Keeping all of the hurt and the pain within me will only allow for a future resurgence. Just as the Sister from Africa learns. And I learn when I punch the walls around me with my fists. It will continually leak its poison into me eventually killing me. Always at a time I am most susceptible to evil taking over and lashing out toward Jesus.

I am told to give all of the pain and hurt inflicted on me by others to Jesus. He will take it anytime you're ready. Place it at the foot of His cross. Place the garbage out and give it to Jesus. I oblige and surrender. I can't be "me" unless I give this away. Forgive like Saint Pope John Paul II, and power awaits. The only way is to ask Mother Mary and keep the Rosary handy.

I go back to grade school. Being bullied. Me being bullied. Definitely not fun for about four years. All of the name calling, the "you're pathetic" looks, the withdrawal from inclusion, and the embarrassment! Not all of the kids I went to grade school with were mean. Just like in everything there are bullies at times. Especially amongst kids. They're all learning how to grow up and be adults. Not always the case, but in essence this is what happens. I admit again, I did it, too!

Jesus helps me to see that I went to grade school with some pretty good kids. We all shared grade school, growing up together. All of the same teachers and their funny little nuances, the same hard tests, to all of the Sacraments within the Catholic Church we received. We all shared Jesus! Hopefully, we all still do! I have to assume most of them grow up and mature, being good productive people with families that love them.

When mom passes, one of my classmates actually shows up to her wake. Even though I hadn't seen him for years, I recognize him right away when he comes up to me. We talk for a while, and I learn he does this for all of his classmates. A very kind and giving soul, spreading his Faith. I am proud to say I shared grade school with him.

Remember when I mention I give the finger to the building of the company that let me go in 2018 when driving by it. Now, it seems rather childish and sophomoric. And then there's the transfer of my wealth to this world because of egregious child support when my daughter wants to live with me. And all the politicians locking me down for an unwarranted amount of time. I have forgiven everyone participating in my downfall, the downfall I let happen, canceling me. They are all God's children, too. I am unaware of all their burdens they are carrying. All in light with the forgiveness of Saint Pope John Paul II and his shooter. I sin, too.

This is what happens when you let Jesus take over. I let it all go. Mother Mary not only leads me back to Her Son, but I can legitimately say in good conscience, "I forgive!" I freely forgive. Can you believe it, "I FORGIVE!" I place all of my pain, sorrow, and hurt at the foot of the cross, "I give it to YOU, Jesus! I surrender. Jesus, I Trust in YOU!"

Also, some beloved co-workers texted me and even showed up to mom's wake. Witnessing all of this support was incredible. Actually, a bit overwhelming in a good way. This all proves to me that people care, and I am definitely on the right track with Jesus. Find the good, and Jesus will find you. I am giving Him the forgiveness and surrender I owe Him.

Being able to forgive includes forgiving yourself. Lord, please have mercy on me, a sinner. A true Act of Contrition places a "wretch" like me inside the grace of Jesus, too. The only thing is I'll change "wretch" to Blessed Child of God. Calling myself a "wretch" is only feeding my unworthiness. The mercy of Jesus is for everyone, no matter what.

Through various sources, I find out that there have been classmates from grade school and high school that have passed. I picture my classmates and me as little children, smiling faces, ready for our life ahead. Just like in yearbook class pictures. It's terribly sad to see. As I think of Patrick, too. And all of their families who love them. Each morning, I include them in my prayers, praying that they all have a path to Heaven. I know Jesus will take care of them all.

See how all of us are interwoven together by each other's actions whether bad or good? Think of a web from a spider, spinning and spinning in a dark basement with little activity. Anyone going down to the basement is covered in clingy, uncomfortable webs. Or, from the love of a grandma, weaving together a warm blanket for her new grandchild. God places us in situations where we share life with certain people. Surrender to God's Will, prove to Him you're onboard with the situation He places you in.

When we take advantage of Mother Mary leading us to Jesus, we're not done. There's some repentance and reparations we must do for our sins, along with forgiving others that have hurt us. Surrender and fully Trust in Jesus. Bind yourself to Him. Pray for the Holy Spirit to dwell within you and your family. Fully accept what the *Seven Gifts of the Holy Spirit* can do for you. Pray for the gifts and an understanding of how to use them the way God wants us to. How will they glorify Him?

Now, we have access to "Fire Power". We as humans have the ability to pray for souls in purgatory, pray for peace, and pray for the living to find Jesus, pray for protection against evil, and pray for people to be healed. All in the name of Jesus. That's what happens when we embrace Jesus. We can even offer up our pain and suffering, requesting Jesus to save souls from the evil of hell. I always include … In the name of Jesus, I declare my Lord, Savior, and King, forever, at the end of all my prayers.

Living souls have this power once they embrace and follow Jesus. This becomes increasingly important for the unborn and the unbaptized. Mother Mary keeps them all close to Her heart, but we in the land of the living must acknowledge them, showing them with our prayers they haven't been forgotten. Pray for them to obtain Heaven soon. With this in mind, we must bear witness to their mothers and the suffering they experience. Remember the mother and her baby are one, no division here.

We as humans have the power to decide our Heaven and Eternity. Souls in purgatory and hell do not. At least with a soul in purgatory, they are promised Heaven once purified. Heaven can't accept a soul without it being clean, but it's up to God's mercy. This is why killing people is wrong. First, it's the Father's calling; secondly, it doesn't give a living soul the opportunity to make their own choice on Heaven and Eternity. It's possible they will make the correct choice over time, and it's possible they may not. That is not for living souls to decide.

White Dove

We like to – kill our Jesus, kill our babies, kill our criminals, kill our innocence, kill our employees, let our old die without dignity, throw away our poor, lie to our children, kill our history, kill our reason, kill our justice, while playing the "Power" of God. We move fast. It's all justified within us. Sounds like we've created hell! Wow, … fire, yes FIRE!

Journal Entry March 2024

When I think of "Fire Power" my mind takes me to military brute force. At times, it is necessary to subdue evil. Nothing better portrays this picture in my mind more than a huge C-130 gunship opening up its gatling gun canons on a designated target when flying high above it. A couple short bursts obliterate everything in its sights. This can sneak up on evil at any time.

God shows us His "Fire Power" in the Bible on multiple occasions in both the Old Testament and the New Testament. **The Ignatius Catholic Study Bible** describes the *"Transfiguration"* of Jesus. Proving God's power in all its splendor and revelation can come down at any time. The Apostles, Peter, James, and John all see and hear this event. They have no idea what Jesus is about to show them

Chapter 5: Fire Power

when He asks them to accompany Him. Matthew describes the momentous scene.

> And after six days Jesus took with him Peter and James and John his brother, and led them up a high mountain apart. And he was transfigured before them, and his face shone like the sun, and his garments became white as light. And behold, there appeared to them Moses and Eli'jah, talking with him. A bright cloud overshadowed them, and a voice from the cloud said, "This is my beloved Son, with whom I am well pleased; listen to him." When the disciples heard this, they fell on their faces, and were filled with awe. But Jesus came and touched them, saying, "Rise, and have no fear."
>
> **Matthew 17:1-7**

In summary, the **Study Bible** explains that God shows the apostles His "Fire Power" on the mountain top. Moses and Eli'jah appear next to Jesus, revealing God's power, as "lawgiver" and "prophet to the New Covenant". Jesus is that New Covenant, the sacrifice. An ideal revelation for the apostles, helping them in their mission after Pentecost.

Or, "Fire Power" can be toned down and portrayed pure as a white dove with a green leaf in its bill flying high above a desecrated area savaged by fire. The wind taking the leaf, placing it inside the desolate, ugly ground. One green leaf fertilizes the onset of vibrant, lush fields once more. This is the "Fire Power" of God our Father when one of His children learns a valuable lesson about this world, relating to Heaven and Eternity.

God is so massive that we can't even imagine the grandeur and the magnificence of our Father. He is pure love and mercy, producing true judgment and justice, too. His children know a bit about all of these elements but can only dig them up as tarnished, broken-up fragments when mining them from the earth.

Time doesn't exist in God, at least the way we know it. We have no control over anything our Father does, … thus our dependence on Him. All of us are only a tiny, miniscule blip in that time. In God time, our problems might be solved with another problem or maybe a fire over a year or two, or it might take decades, or even centuries, or as soon as a second.

Heaven is formed with the Father in mind. It is His. And built to accommodate all of His love and mercy with their accompanying judgment and justice. God says, "Yes!" creating all the angels and Archangels for His court in Heaven and His children on earth out of love. In the environment of Heaven, one always has the choice to love and share in paradise. Saying, "Yes!" is the key to our Father. With this choice, you are embracing Him, accepting His Word, and the plans He has for you. All in order to be with Him in Heaven for Eternity.

Then satan uses his choice, saying, "No!" out of pride or arrogance. No matter, it can't accept the loss of control. The Archangel Michael escorts it out of Heaven. "No!" cannot intermix with the goodness of Heaven's surroundings; it can't. Saying, "No!" equals the opposite of love, which is hate. When embracing this evil, it is burning for eternity surrounded by hate.

Chapter 5: Fire Power

Once kicked out of Heaven, the extension of evil resurfaces on earth. It pounces on all God's creation. Men and women let the serpent in, creating a web of problems and suffering. Since "eating the apple" in the time of Adam and Eve, our knots have only grown larger, tighter and more inter-related around all of us.

We succumb to evil by doing everything as described in my Journal Entry from March 2024 at the beginning of this section. We justify a lot of killing, throwing people away, and lying. In people's minds, the excuses are always "legitimate" in order to get ahead in this world. When we play God, the justification becomes evil. Evil is easy, too easy!

When we need our Father, as we are all dependent on Him, what do we do? Out of more love, He sends us His Son and the Holy Spirit; we have His Mother and the Holy Family; we have all the Saints, the Magisterium of the Catholic Church, the Sacraments, all His graces and blessings, and best of all … His mercy.

His magnificent Self turns into simpler pieces for us to understand. Start with one, grab it. Holding it tightly will eventually lead you to all of them. Again, by choice. Mother Mary will take over and lead you to Jesus.

> Then Jesus told his disciples, "If any man would come after me, let him deny himself and take up his cross and follow me. For whoever would save his life will lose it. For what will it profit a man, if he gains the whole world and forfeits his life? Or what shall a man give in return for his life?
>
> **Matthew 16:24-26**

We begin with Heaven being pure love and mercy. I am a temple of the Lord. We are human and succumb to the evil one and sin. Only a "fiery ordeal" will overturn my tables of corruption in my temple. Mother Mary picks up my pieces, leading me away from evil, toward Her Son. Like only a Mother can. Pushing Her away hurts Her, like it does Jesus. But trust, She always shows up the next morning for Her children with Her foot on the serpent's head.

This is my story of fire. Defined by all the important pieces of my life, sharing their truth with many short clips. Lessons learned in Truth, stringing it all together and defining me now. It begins with fire and ends with the pureness of a white dove carrying a green leaf in its bill. Although I find its meaning and my goal turns into Heaven and Eternity, I am a sinner.

Now I need to put the reader on the spot. I lost everything in this world except my family and our house because of the "fiery ordeal" called Covid-19. But I did gain strength in my Faith. How does it compare to your story, your life? Do your goals fit in more with the world or Heaven and Eternity? Do you trust the world? What pain do you keep locked up inside?

We are all interwoven together by being children of God. We all learn from each other. I'm only attempting to spread what happened to me out of love for everyone. I'm not special and don't have all the answers, but I am your brother. I challenge everyone to listen quietly for answers to these questions. Embrace Our Lady and say the Holy Rosary.

Because I am your brother, I ask Mother Mary to take a couple of your most burdensome worries and intercede for you, helping you through them, … ultimately, finding Jesus in the process. Somehow, some way, find Her Son, Jesus.

This is my Sanctity. If I can find it, you can, too. It's a good start. … Can I keep this gift? Using Peter and Paul and all the Apostles as a template, I will share in spreading the fire, next is Salvation!

www.ingramcontent.com/pod-product-compliance
Lightning Source LLC
Chambersburg PA
CBHW060831050426
42453CB00008B/645